Marx Hardy Defoe Abbott Melville Montaigne Machiavelli Haggard Chesterton Cooper Emerson Joyce Austen Hugo Eliot Grimm Molière Stoker Carroll Christie Wilde Maupassant Byron Schiller Smith Kafka Hall Garnett Goethe Einstein Fitzgerald Engels Hawthorne Dostoyevsky Cotton Kipling Doyle Willis Baum Henry Nietzsche Balzac Leslie Dumas Flaubert Turgenev Stockton Vatsyayana Crane Burroughs Verne Curtis Tocqueville Gogol Vinci Homer Widger Tolstoy Whitman Busch Darwin Thoreau Twain Scott Plato Potter Freud Zola Lawrence Harte Kant Jowett Stevenson Dickens Burton Hesse Andersen London Descartes Cervantes Voltaire Poe Aristotle Wells Hale James Hastings Cooke Bunner Shakespeare Irving Richter Chambers da Shaw Wodehouse Benedict Alcott Doré Dante Chekhov Pushkin Swift Newton

 tredition®

tredition was established in 2006 by Sandra Latusseck and Soenke Schulz. Based in Hamburg, Germany, tredition offers publishing solutions to authors and publishing houses, combined with world-wide distribution of printed and digital book content. tredition is uniquely positioned to enable authors and publishing houses to create books on their own terms and without conventional manu-facturing risks.

For more information please visit: www.tredition.com

TREDITION CLASSICS

This book is part of the TREDITION CLASSICS series. The creators of this series are united by passion for literature and driven by the intention of making all public domain books available in printed format again - worldwide. Most TREDITION CLASSICS titles have been out of print and off the bookstore shelves for decades. At tredition we believe that a great book never goes out of style and that its value is eternal. Several mostly non-profit literature projects provide content to tredition. To support their good work, tredition donates a portion of the proceeds from each sold copy. As a reader of a TREDITION CLASSICS book, you support our mission to save many of the amazing works of world literature from oblivion. See all available books at www.tredition.com.

Project Gutenberg

The content for this book has been graciously provided by Project Gutenberg. Project Gutenberg is a non-profit organization founded by Michael Hart in 1971 at the University of Illinois. The mission of Project Gutenberg is simple: To encourage the creation and distribution of eBooks. Project Gutenberg is the first and largest collection of public domain eBooks.

Color Value

C. R. (Chandler Robbins) Clifford

Imprint

This book is part of TREDITION CLASSICS

Author: C. R. (Chandler Robbins) Clifford
Cover design: Buchgut, Berlin – Germany

Publisher: tredition GmbH, Hamburg - Germany
ISBN: 978-3-8472-1462-5

www.tredition.com
www.tredition.de

Color Value

By C. R. CLIFFORD

Published by CLIFFORD & LAWTON
373 Fourth Avenue, New York

[Pg 2]

Copyrighted, 1907
By Clifford & Lawton

— — —

Fourth Edition

grolier craft press, inc., n. y.

[Pg 3]

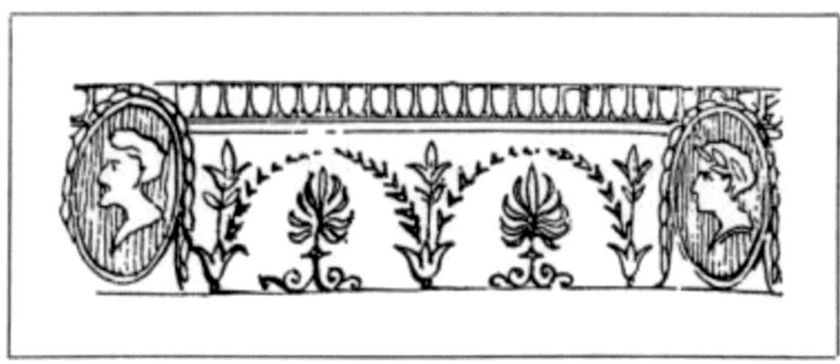

FUNDAMENTAL CONDITIONS

LIGHT, COLOR, FORM, PROPORTION
AND DIMENSIONS

Whatever is good in interior decoration is the result of consistent relationship between Light, Color, Form, Proportion and Dimensions. The choice of Color should be guided by the conditions of Light. The beauty of Form and the symmetry of Proportion can exist only by a balance with Dimensions.

Therefore, apart from any knowledge of historic or period decoration, effective or successful work must observe the technical laws governing conditions.

LIGHT

1. The white light of the sun is compounded of an almost innumerable number of color elements, as shown by the phenomena of the rainbow or by experimenting with the prism. (See ¶ 7.) When a ray of sunshine passes through a glass prism it is decomposed or separated, and if the prismatic colors [Pg 4] are received upon a white screen you will find on the spectrum among the colors generated a pure blue, a pure red and a pure yellow. These are the primary colors, and it is necessary when thinking color to bear these prismatic colors in mind as standards.

2. Color is an internal sensation originating in the excitation of the optic nerve by a wave action which we call light.

3. The theory of light, the wave theory, is based upon the assumption that throughout all space there is an infinitely thin medium called ether. Scientists differ as to what this may be, but its movements constitute light, a reflection from a luminous body.

4. Everything which we see is visible because it either emits light, like a flame, or reflects light.

5. A piece of black cloth upon a white plate reflects but a small proportion of the light. The plate reflects a large proportion. A piece of black velvet reflects less light than black cloth and gives the effect of absolute blackness, or an empty and dark space.

6. In practical demonstrations the study of color will be confusing unless it is understood at the outstart that pure prismatic colors can seldom be found in manufactured pigments, hence any demonstration of the theory of color composition is usually unsatisfactory.

7. The theory which brings out of a ray of sunshine the disunited prismatic colors carries with it the [Pg 5] deduction that before separation these colors constitute white light; but it must be manifest to even the superficial reader that such colors are mere spectrum colors—vision colors—and any amalgamation of material or pigment colors, so far from producing white, produces almost black.

8. The theory that red and yellow make orange, and that a red and blue make violet, is correct; but if one attempts to demonstrate the theory with pigments, one is confronted not only by the lack of

standard manufactured colors but by impurities, adulterations and chemical reaction in the pigments. The adulteration may not be perceptible in one primary color, but it is manifest when that color is brought into action with another primary, for it is seldom that a pure secondary results.

[Pg 6]

COLOR NOMENCLATURE—HARMONIES

9. Color nomenclature includes primary, secondary and tertiary colors, and innumerable hues, shades and tints. All these colors bear relations to one another, either relations of analogy, or relations of contrast. (See ¶ 18 and ¶ 19.)

The Circle Diagram I shows the manner in which the various colors are formed. (See also Diagram III.)

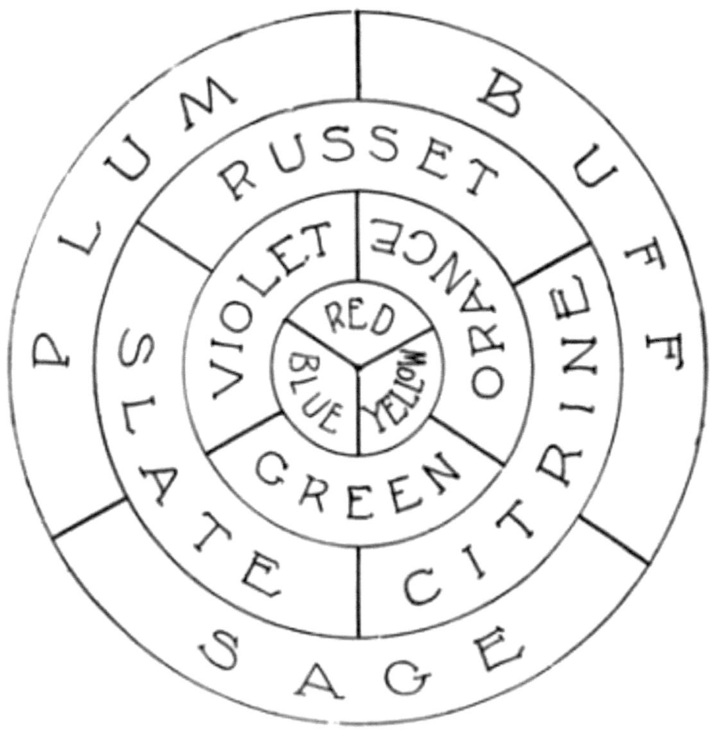

DIAGRAM I

The third circle shows how slate, citrine and [Pg 7] russet are made. For instance, slate is one part of violet and one part of green. Hence, a tertiary color is made of equal parts of two secondaries.

The outer circle, buff, sage and plum, can be analyzed in the same way.

This Diagram I is arranged to show not only component parts of a color, but the parts that properly harmonize.

10. In music it is an established fact that certain notes used in pleasing combination produce sounds we call harmonies. The moment that more than one note is struck, there is danger of discord, and when ten notes resound to the touch of the player, they must be the right notes, or they jar upon the sensibilities. In the use of color the same immutable law applies.

11. In Circle Diagram II the letters RV mean reddish violet, being a violet having more red than blue in its composition. BV means bluish violet, being a violet having more blue than red in its composition. BG means bluish green, being a green having more blue than yellow in its composition. YG means yellow green, being a green having more yellow than blue in its composition. YO means yellowish orange, being an orange having more yellow than red in its composition. RO means reddish orange, being an orange having more red than yellow in its composition. Thus we may advance from red to yellow by graduations almost imperceptible, by [Pg 8] the addition of yellow, to a reddish orange, and so on gradually to orange, continuing on to yellowish orange, finally revealing pure yellow.

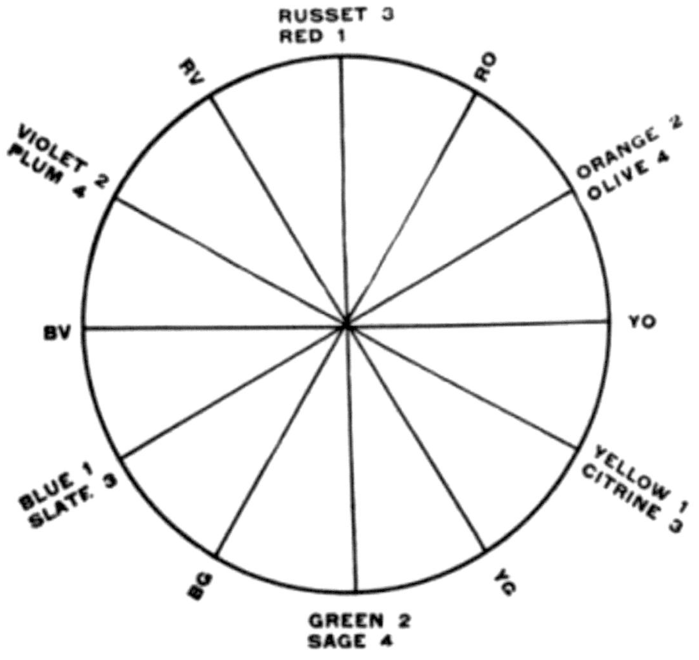

DIAGRAM II

[Pg 9]

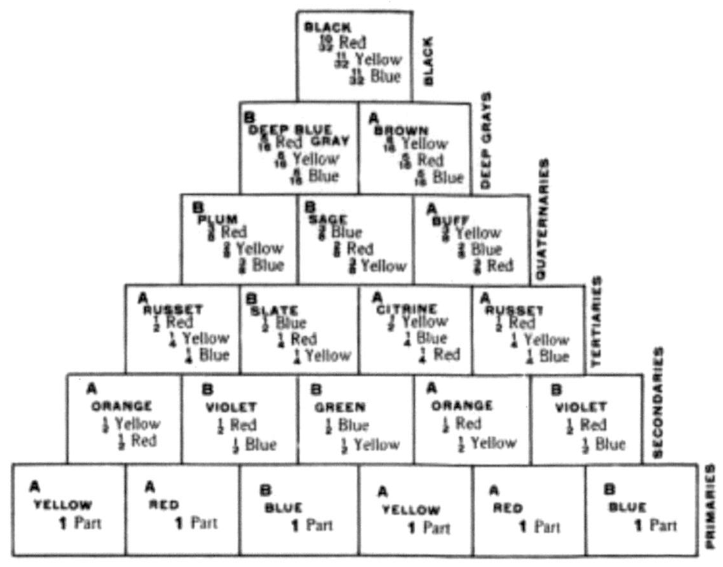

DIAGRAM III

12. The contrasting color at any stage may be determined by proceeding in a direct line across the circle: Red has for its contrasting color green; hence, reddish orange would have for its contrasting color a bluish green, for the simple reason that if [Pg 10] red contrasts with green and orange contrasts with blue, the color between the red and the orange would contrast with the color between the green and the blue. Let us determine the contrasting color for crimson. Crimson is simply a red slightly tinged with blue. If red contrasts with green, a shade a little to the left of red slightly tinged with blue would contrast with a shade a little to the right of green slightly tinged with yellow. In other words, crimson, RV, would contrast with yellowish green, YG. Determine at what point of the circle any color that you have in mind will come, and the contrasting color would be immediately opposite.

13. The harmony of analogy consists of the harmony of related colors or tones of one color. (See ¶ 17.)

14. The harmony of contrast consists of colors in no way related. As an example of the harmony of analogy, we would mention red and orange, because both of these colors have ingredients in common, red being one of the two component parts of orange. As an example of the harmony of contrast, we suggest red and green, because there is nothing in common between the two, red being a primary color, and green a secondary, composed of the other two primaries, yellow and blue. (See ¶ 17.)

15. Green is called the complement of red. The complement of blue would be orange, because [Pg 11] orange is formed by combining the remaining primaries, red and yellow; and the complement of yellow would be violet, because violet is composed of blue and red, the other primaries.

16. In Diagram II we have arranged at opposite points the primaries 1, the secondaries 2, the tertiaries 3, the quaternaries 4.

But Diagram III goes further into the subject.

It is easy to understand the composition of secondaries, but it is not so easy to know the tertiaries and quaternaries. (See also Diagram I.)

CONTRAST ANALOGIES

17. Diagram III is of the utmost value to the colorist, illustrating not only the composition of color, but showing the origin of each secondary from the two primaries, the origin of each tertiary from two secondaries, and of each quaternary from two tertiaries. It shows by groupings the harmonies of analogy or related colors; also the harmonies of contrast: By moving on the board one color on one line to another color upon another line, like the moving of a knight in a game of chess, and confining the moves always to adjoining lines, like yellow to violet, violet to citrine, citrine to plum, plum to brown. Yellow and violet are true contrasts, the one color having nothing in common with the other. The citrine and the plum, however, are approximate contrasts. For greater convenience, we have numbered the contrasting colors A's and B's. Absolute contrast is [Pg 12] where the two colors have nothing in common. For compo-

sition purposes, however, citrine and violet may be considered contrasts, or correctly speaking, contrast analogies. (See ¶ 19.)

18. A harmony of contrast means the utilization of a primary color with its complementary, or a color in conjunction with another color in no degree related: a primary with a secondary. But when we soften these contrasting colors by the addition of white we have in the lighter tints a scale of chroma that is a form of analogy.

19. All combinations of secondary and tertiary colors, while apparently harmonies of contrast (the tertiary being made by the composition of two secondaries), constitute, in fact, contrast analogies, because by analysis we find that all tertiaries possess color components occurring in the apparently contrasting secondaries. (See Diagram III.)

20. The harmony of contrast, literally, can only occur in the pure primary colors juxtaposed to the pure secondary colors, for in no case does the color formed by the combination of the two primaries have anything in common with the third primary; while a tertiary composed of two secondaries invariably has qualities possessed by the third secondary.

21. In a room which is small or dark, the light tints in harmonies of analogy are advisable.

[Pg 13]

PROPORTIONS

22. In the use of one color with another of contrasting character the question frequently arises, what proportion of each should be used to obtain the best effect? Illustrative color books show usually samples of color of the same size, leading one unconsciously to the error that contrasting colors should occupy the same surface dimensions.

23. In every room there must be a prevailing or dominant color, and the use of a contrasting color must be limited to proportions which give simply a pleasing emphasis. Let us assume that a room has a deep frieze pronouncedly green. To treat the rest of the wall in red of a direct contrast would be ineffective.

24. If a rule can be applied we would say that no strong normal color should be used in large surfaces. If we were dealing with pigments we would say that if one-sixth of a side-wall is devoted to a frieze in green, the balance of the wall space should be treated with the same amount of red, mixed with the same amount of gray.

25. For a room that is small and well lighted the fresh tints are not as desirable as the gray shades or tertiaries in conjunction with secondaries.

COLOR IN LARGE OR SMALL ROOMS

26. For a large room well lighted, yellow, red and orange in delicate shades are not as desirable as orange, violet and russet in light shades. This rule, [Pg 14] however, may be reversed for a large room that is dimly lighted.

A superabundance of light gives an uncomfortable glare.

27. One may mechanically obtain harmony of analogy in proper proportions for the treatment of a room or a design by following the guidance of Diagram I. It will be noted in this diagram that the inner circle is blue, red and yellow, the primary colors.

The second circle is composed of the secondaries; the third circle, the tertiaries, and the outer circle, the quaternaries.

There is a nice distinction in the combination of primaries for the formation of secondaries, and exact proportions are quite necessary.

An orange, for instance, would be off shade if it did not consist of half red and half yellow, but in the making of the quaternaries, which are, at best, gray shades, exact proportions are not necessary.

Nevertheless, in Diagram I we have observed exact proportions in order to make our demonstration clear.

The harmony of analogy is the combination of colors related, but the relationship must be displayed in proportions consistent with the origin of each and every color used.

Let us assume that the prevailing note in a room, in either the side-wall or floor, is sage.

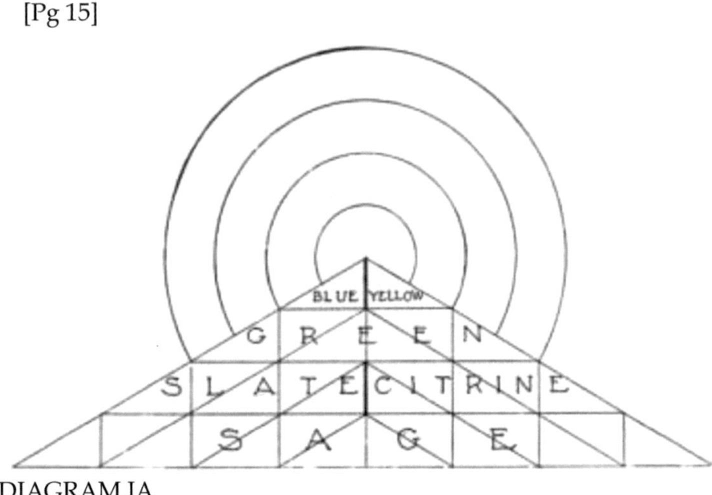

DIAGRAM IA

[Pg 16] We can tell by drawing lines from the center of Diagram I to the extremities of the space marked sage that there is a little blue and a little yellow, some green and slate and citrine used in the composition of sage, and hence the use of these colors constitutes the harmony of relationship or analogy.

COLOR PROPORTIONS

28. But to arrive at proportions we must reduce the circular table to a geometrical table. We must straighten out the lines so that the exact proportions are apparent. We need not confuse the reader by mathematics, but to establish our theory we produce the Diagram IA, and it will be here seen that the relative proportions existing in the segments of the circles have been observed in the triangles.

Thus we have thirty-two right-angled triangles.

Sage occupies fourteen-thirty-seconds of the entire composition; slate occupies five-thirty-seconds; citrine, five-thirty-seconds; green, six-thirty-seconds; blue, one-thirty-second; yellow, one-thirty-second; and these colors, to observe the proper harmony of analogy in a room, should be used in the proportions above indicated.

Sage should be in the preponderance; citrine and slate should occupy nearly one-sixth of the entire composition, green about one-fifth, and the whole should be picked out with touches of sharp blue and sharp yellow, representing each one-thirty-second.

Let us take, for instance, a room that is in white woodwork, and apply the sage to the walls and the slate to the floor, and lighten the sage with citrine [Pg 17] and lighten the slate with violet, and intersperse orange and green in a way permitted by the proportions at our command. When the work is completed we find a harmony of analogy which can be then relieved by touches of the primitive colors, blue and yellow, in the proportions shown.

29. Good examples of contrast color effects may be found in the following series of combinations:

PROPORTIONS OF COLOR ANALYSIS FROM ASSYRIAN TILES.

Example No. 1.

Blue-Green	60
Greenish-Yellow	8
Orange	6
Purple-Brown	6
White	20
	— —
	100

No. 2.

Blue	35
Yellow	30

White	15
Dull Red	10
Black	10
	— —
	100

No. 3.

Blue	60
Deep Yellow	20
Light Yellow	10
White	10
	— —
	100

No. 4.

Pale Yellow	34
Green	27
Blue	25
Red	6
Gold	4
Black	2
White	2
	— —
	100

No. 5.

| Black | 63 |
| Yellow | 17 |

Green		9
Red		4
Light Red		3
Blue		3
White		1
		— —
		100

No. 6.

Green		36
Blue-Green		24
Yellow		14
Red		11
White		10
Dull Red		3
Black		2
		— —
		100

No. 7.

Green		36
Blue-Green		24
Yellow		14
Red		11
White		10
Dull Red		3
Black		2
		— —
		100

[Pg 19]

BLACK—WHITE—GRAY

30. We do not wish to be understood as stating that the work of the colorist is solely mechanical; but we would emphasize that the influences of color are very largely the result of studied proportions. The basis upon which one operates must be soundly constructed upon the theory of scale, and scale is mechanically determined. If red is lightened by the addition of white, or darkened by the addition of black, it is removed to another scale, and can only harmonize by contrast with its complement by adding to green the same amount of white or black that has changed the character of the red, and this should be mathematically accurate.

31. To place white by the side of a color heightens or intensifies the tone of that color. To put black beside a color has the opposite effect. It weakens the color. Every woman looks better in white, hence white is the universal wedding gown, the universal party dress for children, and, wherever practical, the universal Summer dress for adults as well. White is worn universally by men and women next to the face, in collars or in neckwear, and the reason for it is that the contiguous white intensifies whatever color they may possess. Black, on the other hand, lessens the color or lowers its tone.

32. Gray is a medium between the two. While it renders an adjacent color less brilliant, it takes to itself at the same time a tint that is a complement of that adjacent color. In other words, gray by the side of green appears faintly pinkish.

[Pg 20] 33. Black is always desirable as an associate with luminous colors. Black does not associate as well with two colors, one of which is luminous and the other sombre, as when associated with two luminous colors.

ORANGE   YELLOW   YELLOW

BLACK	BLACK	BLACK
RED	ORANGE	RED

YELLOW	GREEN	ORANGE
BLACK	BLACK	BLACK
VIOLET	YELLOW	GREEN

The green being yellowish and the violet reddish.

White is preferable when associated with a luminous and a sombre color. Thus,

RED	ORANGE	RED	YELLOW
WHITE	WHITE	WHITE	WHITE
BLUE	BLUE	VIOLET	BLUE

ORANGE	GREEN	GREEN	YELLOW
WHITE	WHITE	WHITE	WHITE
VIOLET	BLUE	VIOLET	VIOLET

The violet being bluish, the green yellowish.

[Pg 21]

ROOM COMBINATIONS

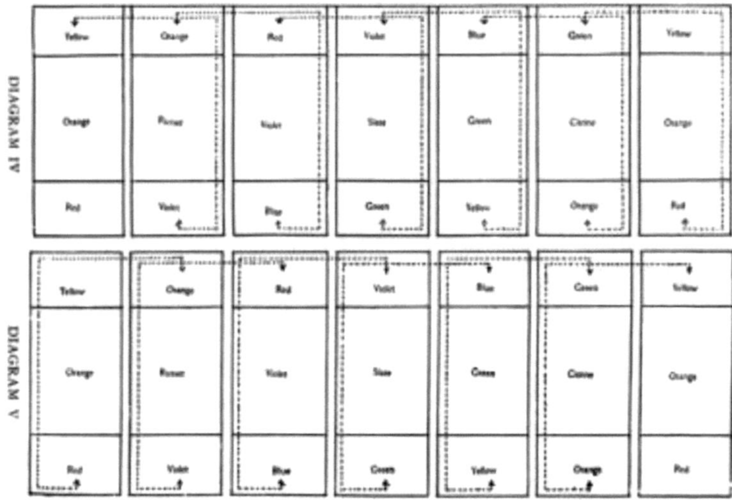

Showing Four-Color Combinations.

[Pg 22]

SEQUENCE OF HARMONIES

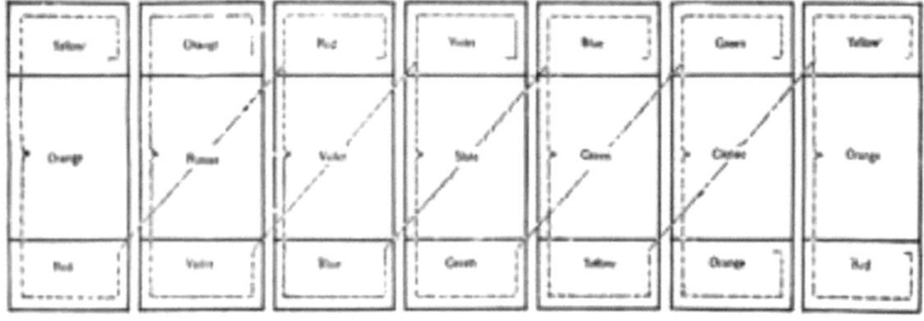

DIAGRAM VI

As these twenty-one sections are arranged, one has the layout for a

suite of
seven
rooms; fol-
lowing the
top line
across in a
light scale,
the harmo-
ny is com-
plete; fol-
lowing the
center line
across in a
normal, the
harmony is
complete;
so also
with the
bottom line
in a lower
scale. Fol-
low the
colors di-
agonally
and you
find they
are repeats,
or very
close to re-
peats—red,
russet, red,
for in-
stance; vio-
let, violet,
violet; blue,
slate, blue;
green,
green,
green; yel-

low,   cit-
rine,   yel-
low;   or-
ange,   or-
ange,   or-
ange.   To
the colorist
the combi-
nations
here   sug-
gested are
full of in-
spiration.

34. The harmony of analogy is a subject that is little understood. It may be color sequence, progression, development or succession.

Thus we may combine red, green and blue by starting with crimson and maintaining the following [Pg 23] sequence: Crimson, red, scarlet, orange, yellow, greenish yellow, green, bluish green, blue, violet, and with added red get back to crimson.

A room or a series of rooms may run to all colors and be still a harmony of analogy if the sequence or succession is gradual.

35. No more delightful harmonies can be imagined than those provided by nature. One may start with the brown of the earth and run into several shades of green, and from that touch upon yellow, and from yellow to orange, and from orange to red, and red to violet, and violet to the blue of the sky. Or one may follow the colorings and the proportion of colorings in flora and never go astray. (See ¶ 22.)

36. In the application of color to the home nothing is more pleasing than the harmony of sequence; the coloring of all rooms must be in sympathy with contiguous rooms. (Diagram VII.) (See ¶ 34.)

37. All rooms are subject to the influence of a north or a south light, or much or little light, and the colorings must be considered accordingly. The ceiling and the upper parts of a wall require more pale colors where more light is needed. On the floor, however,

where the greatest light falls, a little black may be added to soften the tone.

38. Red and green are sharply contrasting colors; violet and yellow and blue and orange sharply contrast, and while their combinations may be used in adjoining [Pg 24] rooms, it will be seen that in Diagram IV these contrasting tones are not in contact, but by their arrangement form analogies of contrast combinations.

39. Yellow, orange, red, violet, blue and green are related; orange, russet, violet, slate, green and citrine are related; red, violet, blue, green, yellow and orange are related. Viewing the ceilings, the side-walls or the floor, there is the harmony of progression that we observe in the tinting of a flower. Viewed collectively the harmony is the same.

40. To illustrate further our point we would take the ceiling line. We start with yellow, a primary color; orange possesses yellow; orange likewise possesses red, the adjoining color; violet possesses red, and it likewise possesses blue. On the side-wall, russet possesses orange, and it also possesses violet; it is the tertiary color made of these two secondaries. Slate is made of green and violet, and is thus also related to citrine.

We do not wish it understood that these colors are to be applied flat, but simply in the predominating expression. (See ¶ 27.)

41. The value of the diagram is obvious when one considers that in no particular is there a break in the sequence; but if we wish a harmony of analogy in a room, or a harmony of related parts, and wish the adjoining room to be in absolute contrast, we simply adopt the red, violet and blue for one room, and the green, citrine and orange for another; or the orange, [Pg 25] russet and violet for one room, and the blue, green and yellow for the other. If, however, the sequence of color is desirable where we move from one apartment to another, and the eye is pleased by a gradual changing color, we can adopt any of these combinations in the order as presented.

42. A vital point in the use of color, regarded usually with indifference or totally misunderstood, is the Unity of Composition to be preserved in the treatment of a series of *floors* in a house; for on each floor of a house the conditions of light vary. As we ascend the stairs

we find each floor requires an altered treatment, because of the added light given from the skylight. (See ¶ 37.) Moreover, in the arrangement of a floor the relation of one room to another is frequently so influential that no one room should be treated without due consideration to the adjacent apartment. (See Diagram VIII.)

Too frequently the whole question of color is dismissed when the matter of north or south exposure is discovered, but the north room on the lower floor of a house is by no means so well lighted as the north room of the fourth or fifth floor, and the scale of color which would lend warmth to such a room would be weak in a more exposed apartment. (See ¶ 30.)

43. Where the artist has but one room to consider there is little scope for his application of color knowledge. He must frequently compromise to meet the conditions. But presuming that he must treat a floor through, he should adopt a Unity which will apply harmoniously to all the rooms and hallways.

[Pg 26]

DIAGRAM VII

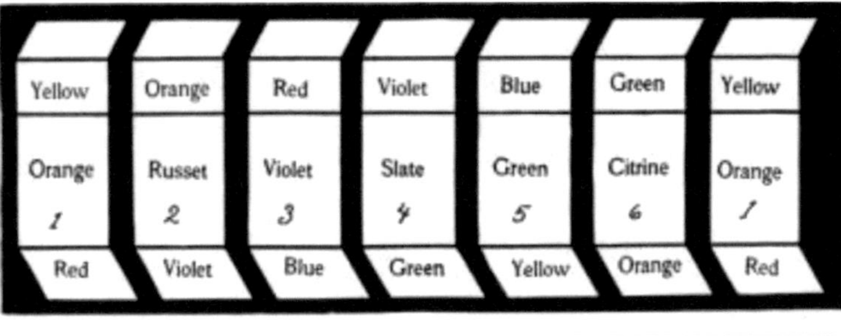

DIAGRAM VIII

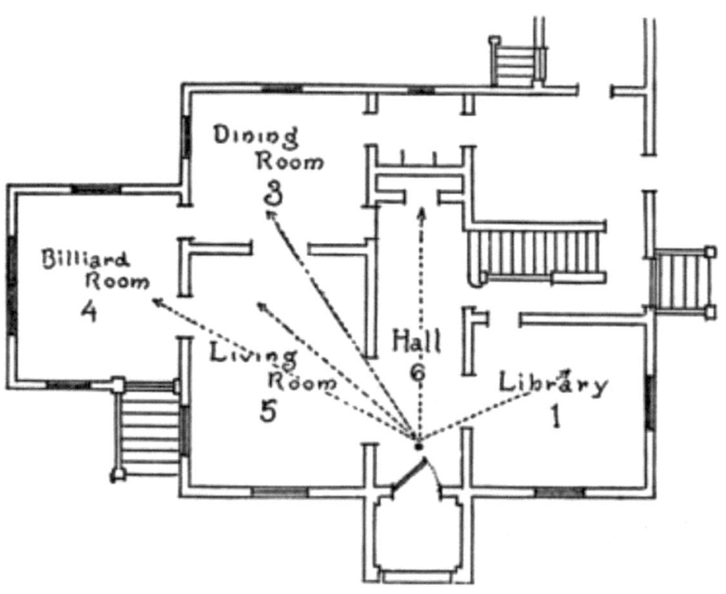

DIAGRAM IX
For Key to Numbers see Diagram VII.

[Pg 28]

CONTIGUOUS HARMONIES

44. For the lower floor he must arrange his colors so that while they moderate the direct glare of a sunny exposure or brighten the cheerlessness of a north light, they will also form a composition that pleases when seen from a point of common observation.

45. On the upper floors the scale of color should be gradually softened, for the yellow or ivory tints that are pleasing on the first floor would be harsh and glaring where there is greater light. Exterior conditions must be borne always in mind.

46. Recalling that the primary colors are yellow, red and blue, and that the secondary colors are orange, violet and green, and that the

tertiary colors are russet, slate and citrine, all with many tints and shades, let us arrange a series of five rooms seriatim, so treating ceiling, side-wall and floor (See Diagram IX) that in passing from one room to another they will be in sequence of color harmony — each complete from floor to ceiling and all in harmony along the ceiling lines, the wall lines and the floor lines.

Let us take the suite of rooms suggested in Diagram IX. We must consider desirable colorings in all of the rooms to be treated, and so far as possible adjust the sequence of treatments, as shown in Diagram VIII, so that the approach to each room will be in harmonious order as viewed from any room. We have five rooms to treat. The library happens to be [Pg 29] on the north side, hence we wish to treat it in colorings that supply the deficiency of sunshine. The hallway is rather dark. The living-room has only one window, and requires more warmth of color than the billiard-room and dining-room, which being sunshiny can be treated in more sombre tones. Therefore we select combination 6 for the hallway. The one room on the right we treat in No. 1. The rooms on the left we treat in Nos. 5, 4 and 3. We have, therefore, as we stand in room No. 6, treated in green, citrine and orange, a view to the right of yellow, orange and red, which is in harmonious juxtaposition. To the left we have a glimpse of rooms, the floors of which adjoining the orange floor of the entrance hall, are yellow, green and blue. The wall spaces adjoining the citrine wall space of the hall treatment are green, slate and violet. The frieze lines adjoining the green of the hall treatment are blue, violet and red — all juxtaposed harmonies. The floors of all rooms are of one deep scale; the walls lighter scale; the friezes and ceiling still lighter. If viewed from room 4 the harmonies are equally effective.

47. Diagram VII is useful for many reasons. In its present shape it shows the harmonies of analogy or related parts. To arrange harmonies of contrast, combine the colors of the first room with the fourth room, the colors of the second room with the fifth room, the colors of the third room with the sixth room. (See ¶ 37.)

48. The floor should usually enter into the color [Pg 30] scheme as the low note in the scale. It is the background for the furniture, and should be deeper than the dado or wainscoting. The wood trims — baseboard, doors, plate-rails, and everything of that character, except the picture molding — should be like the woodwork of the furniture. This brings the woodwork into contrast with the wainscoting (unless the wainscoting be wood) and into harmony with the side-walls, although the degree of harmony is far removed. Thus, if the woodwork of the furniture is mahogany, the wainscoting green, the side-walls pink and gray, we would find the window trims of mahogany, or imitation mahogany, in harmony with the side-walls. (See ¶ 51 and ¶ 52.)

49. I would lay down the rule that the wood trims of a room should harmonize by analogy with the side-walls where such walls are provided with a contrasting wainscoting; but if there is no wainscoting, or the wainscoting be also of wood, then the wood trims and furniture contrast with the side-wall.

Substitute green side-wall for the pink, ¶ 48.

White woodwork is always permissible. Study Diagram VI on page 22.

50. The picture molding may harmonize with the ceiling. Indeed, a white picture molding frequently is better than one matching the general woodwork (See ¶ 37); a dark upper molding, moreover, reduces the apparent size of a room.

51. Where black furniture is used, or gold [Pg 31] furniture, it will of course be understood that the wood trims shall not be black or gold; but so long as they are in harmony, that will be sufficient. White wood trims are nearly always permissible as a substitute for colored wood.

52. Tones of gray with soft colorings (See ¶ 32), are always safe.

To summarize (Note ¶ 37):

53. In harmonies of contrast the side-walls, the furniture woodwork, wood trimming, cove, ceiling and the curtains should be related.

54. The rugs, frieze, wainscoting or dado, furniture upholsterings and the curtain borders should be related. (See ¶ 49.)

55. If the curtains have no borders, then the curtains contrast with the wood trims.

56. Remember always cove and ceiling should be the palest tint of the side-wall color, and the rug should be of the deepest contrast to the side-wall, in harmony with the wainscoting, if there is a wainscoting. Remember, also, that the colors here prescribed are never to be of the same scale. The rug or carpet is of the deepest, and the ceiling of the palest. While certain colors are to contrast, they are not to contrast in the same scale. (See ¶ 37 and ¶ 40.)

57. If we find that the tone of color of the wainscoting, for instance, is a bluish green, the side-wall should be of a reddish orange; for the reason that if green contrasts with red, and if blue contrasts with [Pg 32] orange, a bluish green would contrast with a reddish orange.

58. Exception to ¶ 56. Only large or well-proportioned rooms can stand the diminishing or reduction effects of contrast. In low ceiling rooms, leave out the contrasting frieze, and let border, cornice and ceiling be in receding colors. (See ¶ 89.)

59. We all know that a northern exposure gives a room a deficiency of sunlight, and the wall treatment should supply this. A southern room, on the other hand, gives so much sunlight that counteracting wall treatments in cold color are permissible.

60. In the color treatment of a room one has either to adopt a harmony of analogy or a harmony of contrast, and this is a matter which depends upon so many conditions that it should be carefully considered. (See ¶ 88 and ¶ 89.) Where a plate-rail is used one must remember that a great deal of color may be furnished by the bric-à-brac, and that the wall behind this plate-rail should be of a color in contrast to the contents of the plate-rail.

61. When we follow a scheme of *contrast* the borders should be usually complements, and if the reader has studied our diagram he will very readily understand how to determine the exact complementary color.

WALL PROPORTIONS

62. The wainscoting or dado should be the same as the top border or frieze, but of a darker tone. The intermixture of white or black is always permissible; [Pg 33] thus a paper as a side-wall might have as its frieze the complementary coloring with more white, while the wainscoting or dado should be the complementary with black added.

63. The cornice should be lighter than the border, and its members may show several tints, with the ceiling lighter still. (See ¶ 92.)

64. As a rule the color of the chair coverings should be the complementary of the side-walls, and the color of the furniture frames should be complementary to the wainscoting; so by following this rule we find that the wainscoting serves as a contrasting background to the chair frame.

65. Let us imagine a room wherein the side-walls are of a reddish tint; the wainscoting, being a complementary color, is of a greenish cast. The furniture is of mahogany, and in contrast to the wainscoting, while the chair covering, being greenish in contrast to the chair frame, is also in contrast to the side-wall. Here we have, then, the color relations of side-wall, wainscoting, furniture-frames and covering; but it is undesirable that these tones should be in the same scale. (See ¶ 62 and ¶ 92, also tables pages 42 and 43.)

[Pg 34]

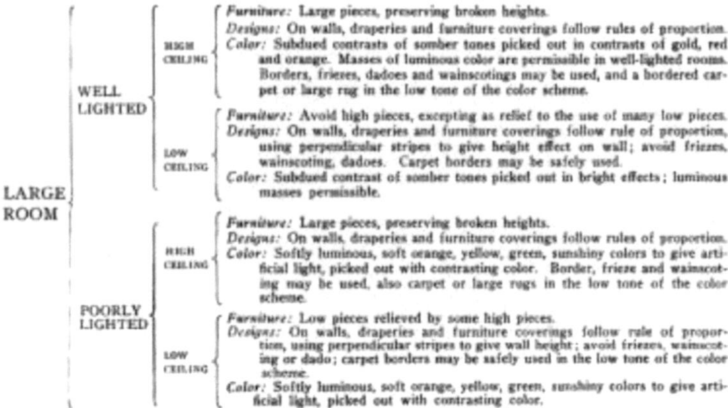

LARGE ROOM

WELL LIGHTED — HIGH CEILING

Furniture: Large pieces, preserving broken heights.
Designs: On walls, draperies and furniture coverings follow rules of proportion.
Color: Subdued contrasts of somber tones picked out in contrasts of gold, red and orange. Masses of luminous color are permissible in well-lighted rooms. Borders, friezes, dadoes and wainscotings may be used, and a bordered carpet or large rug in the low tone of the color scheme.

WELL LIGHTED — LOW CEILING

Furniture: Avoid high pieces, excepting as relief to the use of many low pieces.
Designs: On walls, draperies and furniture coverings follow rule of proportion, using perpendicular stripes to give height effect on wall; avoid friezes, wainscoting, dadoes. Carpet borders may be safely used.
Color: Subdued contrast of somber tones picked out in bright effects; luminous masses permissible.

POORLY LIGHTED — HIGH CEILING

Furniture: Large pieces, preserving broken heights.
Designs: On walls, draperies and furniture coverings follow rules of proportion.
Color: Softly luminous, soft orange, yellow, green, sunshiny colors to give artificial light, picked out with contrasting color. Border, frieze and wainscoting may be used, also carpet or large rugs in the low tone of the color scheme.

POORLY LIGHTED — LOW CEILING

Furniture: Low pieces relieved by some high pieces.
Designs: On walls, draperies and furniture coverings follow rule of proportion, using perpendicular stripes to give wall height; avoid friezes, wainscoting or dado; carpet borders may be safely used in the low tone of the color scheme.
Color: Softly luminous, soft orange, yellow, green, sunshiny colors to give artificial light, picked out with contrasting color.

[Pg 35]

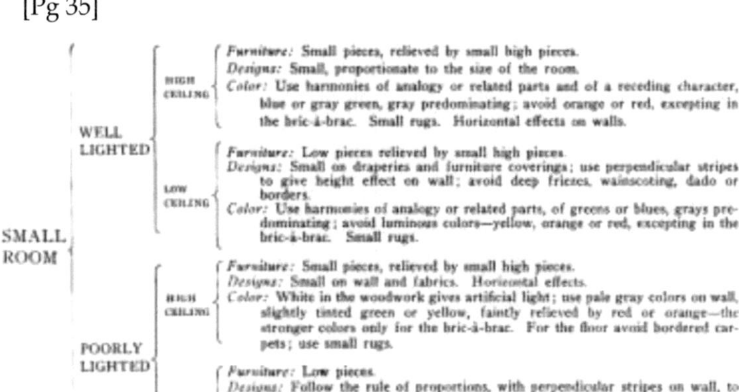

SMALL ROOM

WELL LIGHTED — HIGH CEILING

Furniture: Small pieces, relieved by small high pieces.
Designs: Small, proportionate to the size of the room.
Color: Use harmonies of analogy or related parts and of a receding character, blue or gray green, gray predominating; avoid orange or red, excepting in the bric-à-brac. Small rugs. Horizontal effects on walls.

WELL LIGHTED — LOW CEILING

Furniture: Low pieces relieved by small high pieces.
Designs: Small on draperies and furniture coverings; use perpendicular stripes to give height effect on wall; avoid deep friezes, wainscoting, dado or borders.
Color: Use harmonies of analogy or related parts, of greens or blues, grays predominating; avoid luminous colors—yellow, orange or red, excepting in the bric-à-brac. Small rugs.

POORLY LIGHTED — HIGH CEILING

Furniture: Small pieces, relieved by small high pieces.
Designs: Small on wall and fabrics. Horizontal effects.
Color: White in the woodwork gives artificial light; use pale gray colors on wall, slightly tinted green or yellow, faintly relieved by red or orange—the stronger colors only for the bric-à-brac. For the floor avoid bordered carpets; use small rugs.

POORLY LIGHTED — LOW CEILING

Furniture: Low pieces.
Designs: Follow the rule of proportions, with perpendicular stripes on wall, to give height effect. Avoid borders on wall; use small rugs on floor.
Color: A preponderance of white in woodwork and fresh gray on wall with a touch of yellow and green in soft tones. Contrasting colors only in bric-à-brac and small details.

[Pg 36]

ROOM PROPORTIONS

66. In small rooms harmonies of contrast are unsafe, because contrasts must involve advancing colors, which make a room look smaller. (See ¶ 86 and ¶ 90.) Harmonies of analogy are far better; and as frieze, wainscoting and dado are not recommended in the

small room, we suggest that the furniture woodwork and the wood trims should be of one color note, unless it is desired that the wood trims should be white; and that the side-walls, curtains and chair upholsterings should be of a note in some degree related and of receding color, picked out with just a touch of contrasting color. (See ¶ 90 and ¶ 91.)

This contrasting color may be introduced in the accessories, the pictures, bric-à-brac, flowers (natural or artificial) or books.

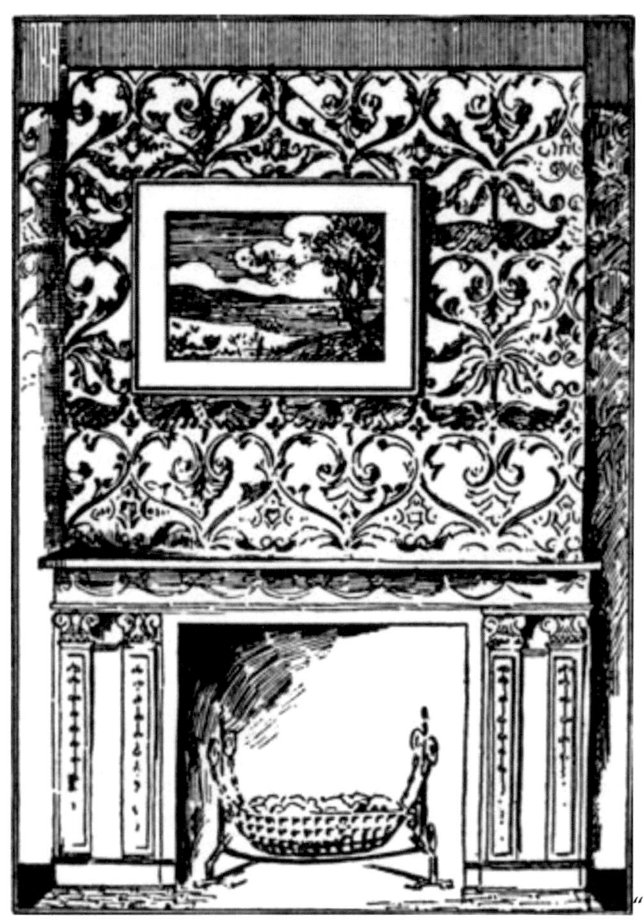

"... pro-
nounced patterns must balance," etc.
(See page 38.)

[Pg 37]

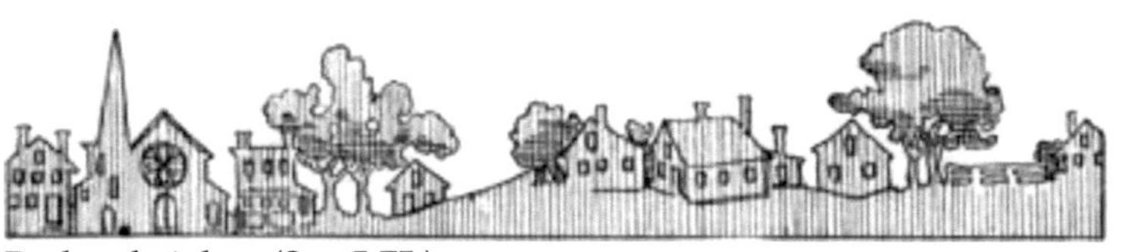

Broken heights. (See ¶ 75.)

DECORATIVE PROPORTIONS

(SEE CHART)

On the preceding pages we present a quick-reference chart of rules that should be followed in furnishing rooms under various conditions of Light and Proportion.

67. A large room with high ceiling and well lighted.
68. A large room with low ceiling and well lighted.
69. A large room with high ceiling and poorly lighted.
70. A large room with low ceiling and poorly lighted.
71. A small room with high ceiling and well lighted.
72. A small room with low ceiling and well lighted.
73. A small room with high ceiling and poorly lighted.
74. A small room with low ceiling and poorly lighted.

There are two considerations to bear uppermost in mind: Proportions affected by Color and Proportions affected by Design.

75. It is easily understood that a large room may be safely furnished with large pieces of furniture, but where there is a wide expanse of floor space care must be exercised to secure broken heights: In a high-ceilinged room the furniture must not be all high; in a low-ceilinged room the furniture must not be all low.

[Pg 38] Avoid straight line effects in the furniture heights and in the wall-paper, which, if in pronounced patterns, must balance in conspicuous wall members and show the broken junctures or bad matchings in inconspicuous or obscure corners.

COLORS THAT GIVE SIZE TO A ROOM

76. The wall and fabric designs must be of a size proportionate to the size of the room. The color treatment of a well-lighted room must be subdued to offset the glare of the natural illumination, and the natural illumination be subdued to soften the color treatment; glare must be avoided.

77. Advancing colors are colors which contain red or yellow in the ascendancy; *receding* colors are those which contain blue in the ascendancy. Green in its purity, being half yellow and half blue, is almost neutral. In the same way violet, being made up of half red and half blue, is theoretically neutral, although the blue tone is usually more assertive than the red and makes the color recede. Any color or hue possesses advancing or receding qualities according to the ascendancy of red, blue or yellow in its composition.

78. Orange is an advancing color; so also is violet in the shades approaching red; green in the shades approaching yellow.

79. Of the tertiary colors russet is an advancing color, because while it contains some blue in the violet of its composition, it contains a preponderance of red and orange.

[Pg 39]

ADVANCING AND RECEDING COLORS

80. Citrine is an advancing color, because while it contains some blue in the green of its composition, it contains a preponderance of yellow and orange; slate is a receding color, because while it contains some yellow in the green of its composition, it contains a preponderance of blue; in the same way plum may be regarded as an advancing color, because of its preponderance of red; buff is an advancing color, because of its preponderance of yellow; sage is a receding color, because of its preponderance of blue.

81. The carpet should always be in the low tone, and in a small room a bordered carpet should be always tabooed. So also should one avoid the use of one rug so placed that a border of woodwork shows around it, because this gives the border effect and makes a small floor space look still smaller. Better use small rugs. The use of a lot of narrow rugs lengthwise along a narrow room will make the room look all the narrower, but the same rugs placed crosswise would make a room look wider.

The diagrams which we have prepared will give even the man who understands it all a quicker grasp of the points involved.

82. Width effect and distance effect are obtained best by arranging the smaller pieces at the farthest points.

83. It is the same with pictures. While a room should be balanced, and the pictures placed in a manner to give this result, it is best, where possible, to [Pg 40] keep the larger pictures, larger effects, always near the eye. The crowding of large pieces at the farthest point diminishes the apparent size of the room.

FLOOR TREATMENTS

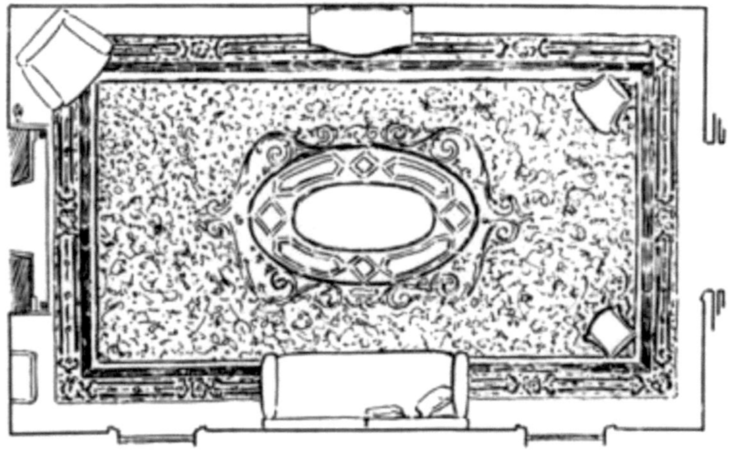

84. Continuous design in ceiling or carpet weakens the size effect; hence rugs which break the continuity by being laid across the room instead of lengthwise are preferable. (See Diagrams and ¶ 81.)

85. It is a safe rule to do a small or narrow room in harmonies of analogy or related colors, colors of a light tone and of receding character. Apart from any effect which color may possess decoratively or pictorially, its value cannot be overestimated in its application to the laws of proportion.

[Pg 41]

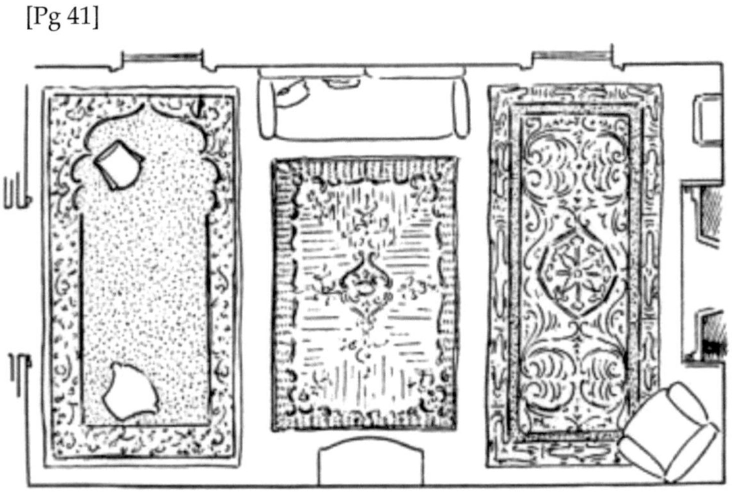

86. Borders may be safely used on the wall or on the carpet of any large room with high ceiling, but wall friezes should be avoided where the ceilings are low, for they foreshorten the height effect.

87. We would avoid borders on the floor of a small room to make it look larger, and we would use wide borders in a large room with a low ceiling so that the floor may be foreshortened.

88. One may utilize in a large, poorly lighted room masses of luminous colors to give artificial sunlight to the room deficient therein, but in the small, poorly lighted room this treatment should be avoided.

[Pg 42]

COLOR SCHEMES FOR ROOMS UNDER NORMAL CONDITIONS

(TN: left page of two page table)

				KEYNOTE COLORS	
A	**B**	**A**	**B**	**A**	**B**
Floor	*Drapery Border*	*Wood Trim*	*Wainscoting*	*Side-Wall*	*Furniture Coverings*
(*Brown and gray tones*)	(*Full tones*)	(*Wood tones*)	(*Deep tones*)	(*Soft tones*)	(*Soft tones*)
Brown	Yellow	Mission	Green	Red	Green
Deep oak brown	Orange	Mission	Blue	Orange	Blue
Light oak	Green	Light oak	Violet	Yellow	Violet
Deep olive	Blue	Oak	Red	Green	Red
Mission tones of slate	Violet	Mahogany	Orange	Blue	Orange
Deep plum	Red	Violet toned or tulip	Yellow	Violet	Yellow

(TN: right page of two page table)

A	**B**	**A**	**B**	**A**

39

Furniture	Frieze	Draperies	Ceiling	Cornice
(*Wood tones*)	(*Soft tones*)	(*Full tones*)	(*Pale wash tones*)	(*Pale wash tones*)
Mahogany	Pale green	Red	Palest green	Pale yellow
Deep oak	Blue	Orange	Palest blue	Pale green
Gold, gray or yellow	Violet	Yellow	Palest violet	Pale blue
Walnut gray	Grayish red	Green	Palest red	Pale violet
Mission brown	Gray orange	Blue	Palest orange	Pale orange
Gold or violet tone	Yellow	Violet	Palest yellow	Pale pink

Exception 1. The ceiling, where there is no pronounced cornice or cove, should follow the wall tint.

Exception 2. Independent of rule, a low ceiling should be in receding color.

It is impossible to tabulate directions for using color without an understanding of the conditions, the size, light and height of a room. (See pages 34 and 35.) The above tables relate only to normal conditions.

White woodwork can be used effectively in the trims of a room and give greater light and size. The darker the wood trims the smaller the room appears. We have left out of consideration the window treatments which, as a rule, should be of white lace, perhaps overdraped in colored stuffs. If the room is poorly lighted, it is obviously undesirable to cut off any light from the window by even laces; the curtains, therefore, in a poorly lighted room should be draped back. Colored laces, grenadines or madras stuffs are frequently used to give period style or color tone, and [Pg 43] wherever they are used, such curtains should harmonize with the wall. So also with the overdraperies to the lace curtains.

89. Luminous or advancing colors make a small room look all the smaller; therefore in small rooms we suggest the use of white woodwork, and in the color treatment we would avoid contrasts, but would suggest harmonies of analogy in receding colors, soft grays, greens and blues. These are not luminous colors and will make a small room look the larger, while the white will give light effects, and if the room appears a trifle somber it can be easily relieved by [Pg 44] the bright colors of the bric-à-brac and by a touch of gold here and there on the wall. (See ¶ 66 and ¶ 85.)

90. There are cases where a small room has a northern exposure, and while apparently expedient to treat such a room in warm colors to supply the deficiency of sunlight, such a course would make a room look smaller.

91. Under the circumstances treat the room in light hues, gray preferred, and get the deficiency of sunlight through some warm isolated details and in the lace curtains.

THE WALL THE KEYNOTE COLOR

92. Our theory of color as applied to room furnishings provides always that the side-wall is the keynote and this keynote is usually fixed for practical reasons in sympathy with the furniture; above to the ceiling's center the note ascends and below to the floor center it descends; it goes into tints as it ascends and into deeper shades of gray and brown as it descends.

If, for instance, blue is the keynote, by adding black you have drabs, slates or grays for the floor, while if the keynote be red you have écrus and browns for the floor light or gray, according to the color scale of the keynote.

93. It must be understood that in designating a color we do not mean that it shall be solid or pure, but merely that it prevails. (See ¶ 29.)

A side-wall may be treated in several colors, but as long as orange prevails, it follows the conditions of [Pg 45] the combination, pages

42 and 43. The factors included in the line designated A are all of one color family. The factors indicated by B are also family colors. It will be seen that the A or B colors taken by themselves form harmonies of analogy; it is only by combining the A's with the B's that we have harmonies of contrast.

If a room is to be done in harmonies of analogy, use the A colors alone or the B colors alone, but never A and B together.

THE PSYCHOLOGY OF COLOR

94. Whatever may be the charm conveyed by design there is a reason for it. We can analyze it.

It has an inherent quality of beauty or historic interest, and there is a definite and distinct reason for our liking it.

But the effect of color is exciting or disturbing, tranquilizing or pleasing, inexplicable and inexpressible, affecting the senses like an appeal to the passions or the appetite. One might as well explain the love of sport, literature, art or vice. The sense of color is a nerve sense, and this sense varies in the individual. We know that colors which are strongest in direct sun rays, like red and orange, arouse the normal senses, while the blues and violets quiet.

Nature provides vast fields of green because favorable in its effects upon humanity. Experiments prove that men of extreme sensibility exposed to the influences of red light finally show excitement which gives muscular development fifty per cent. in excess of the power possessed by the same subject when [Pg 46] exposed for the same period under the influences of blue light.

TO DETERMINE THE COLOR SENSE

Color, like music, while subjected to positive rules of harmony, appeals to natures according to the responsiveness of their nerve sense, and the practical decorator in dealing with a customer should discover at the outstart the character of that nerve sense. Some natures respond to the normal colors, barbaric colors. Some respond to the softer tints and are disturbed by the sharper tones. A dulled sense requires sharp contrasts; a quickened sense is satisfied with the soft gray tones. Apart from any question of propriety or environment the individual taste for color must be determined before the individual taste can be pleased.

A demonstration of four examples in color may serve the purpose of determining one's color sense.

First. Combinations of normal primary and secondary colors, (*a*) arranged in contrasts, (*b*) in analogies.

Second. Combinations of tones of the above colors, (*a*) arranged in contrasts, (*b*) in analogies.

Third. Combinations of tints of the above colors, (*a*) arranged in contrasts, (*b*) in analogies.

Fourth. Combinations of the gray (tertiary) tones of the above colors, (*a*) arranged in contrasts, (*b*) in analogies.

95. Do not allow your personal color-sympathies to dominate your work. All colors have their usefulness, for there are occasions when it is proper they [Pg 47] should be used, apart from any question of harmony; one must consider always the uses of colors, the lights, and the purpose of the room under treatment.

96. Nature gives to the dark forest depths great brilliancy of floriculture, and dark-skinned people indulge unconsciously the same bright scale of color. But as we come out of the forest and advance in civilization we use barbaric colorings more discriminately.

97. We employ gold, orange or yellow for the north room not for inherent beauty, but for the sense of warmth which they convey to an atmosphere chilled by the absence of sunlight. We employ receding colors in a small room that the room may look larger. We employ cold colors in a sunny room, especially in the summer home, for reasons psychological rather than æsthetic.

PERIOD USES OF COLOR

98. If our furniture is white and gold, it is clearly evident that the colorings of a room should be soft and harmonious. If we adopt the dark teakwood of India or the deep brown of Flanders, our color scheme again changes. The preponderance of white in Colonial

rooms was due to architectural conditions. White illuminates; and in the days when our ceilings were no higher than seven and a half feet, and our windows were small, the room needed an artificial light, and white supplied this.

99. In furnishing an Empire room, the decorators have, little by little, led themselves to believe that [Pg 48] what is known as Empire green is a distinct shade of green. On the contrary, green was used in the period of the Empire simply because it was in pleasing contrast with the mahogany and brass so much used. If the mahogany is dark, a dark green is desirable; if light, a light green.

100. Egyptian decoration was full of gold and brilliant coloring, and a popular form of combination was the triad form:

> Black, yellow and red.
> Red, blue and white.
> Dark blue, light blue and white.
> Cream color, blue and black.
> Dark red, medium yellow and blue.

101. The Greek decorators, who painted in fresco, used white, red, blue, yellow and black. Natural marbles were much used in green and red and alabaster, and bronze, gold and silver.

We see the flat colors of the Greek, Etruscan and Pompeiian age and we imagine they are typical of the period, but we must consider that the examples of that period which we now possess are faded and emasculated, and that the more authentic the example, the more aged it is, and hence the more weakened in color character.

The Greeks loved color, and their embroideries were in gold and blue and Tyrian purple.

Roman coloring was but a continuance of the Greek, characterized by dark and rich backgrounds, which were frequently black, red or deep yellow and [Pg 49] dark blue, on which figures and landscapes, or animals, or groups from still life, were executed in bright colorings of powerful contrasts. Black and white were used, and later, when the Byzantine artists and craftsmen found their way to Western Italy, they spread this love of bold coloring, so that at the dawn of the Renaissance we find a return to the Greek and Roman coloring, which, however, was modified in England, Germany and Flanders, according to temperamental conditions.

102. We find, for instance, some forms of Florentine decoration, full of yellow, red-yellow, blue-greens and light slate blues. Botticelli used whites, creams, reds and citrine, with umber tones heightened by gold, and if we examine carefully the Sixteenth and Seventeenth Century Italian brocades which are preserved in the museums, we discover a great preponderance of yellow-green as an ornament on dark violet, or light olive green on dark blue, or dull orange on crimson brown.

In some of the richest early Italian fabrics we find:

Purple and sage-green ornaments on indigo ground; outlines in gold.

Dull crimson, pale blue and chrome yellow ornaments on dark gray ground.

Pale yellow-green ornaments on deep amber ground.

Dark blue-green and light greenish-yellow ornaments on deep crimson ground.

Pale greenish-blue ornaments on dark gray-blue ground, with white and gold picked out in small quantities.

Emerald green and dull orange ornaments on dark gray-green ground outlined in gold.

[Pg 50]

103. The French Renaissance takes inspiration from the Roman and Greek.

The Louis XIV is a development of the Renaissance, with a conspicuous use of gold.

The Louis XV is an elaboration along the same lines.

The Louis XVI is a simplification and a return to the classic.

The Georgian is largely Roman and Pompeiian.

104. The Adam style was taken directly from the Pompeiian, but in most cases, instead of having the Pompeiian solid color background with design lightly executed, the background is in the light color, and the design dark. To follow strictly the Pompeiian palace style would be too garish in our modern circumscribed environment.

105. It is a nice psychological problem to decorate the house in a way to give true balance to the æsthetic sense. No matter how great one's admiration for a thing, there is always a final point of satiety at which the desire needs rest or balance. A woman may love flowers, for example, but in the season of flowers, when all nature supplies an over-abundance, the visual sense becomes satiated, and the house interior that is furnished in cool tints and two-tones gives positive relief.

106. On the other hand, floral decorations in the home are the balance needed to the mind that craves them during the Winter period when there is a lack of color without.

[Pg 51]

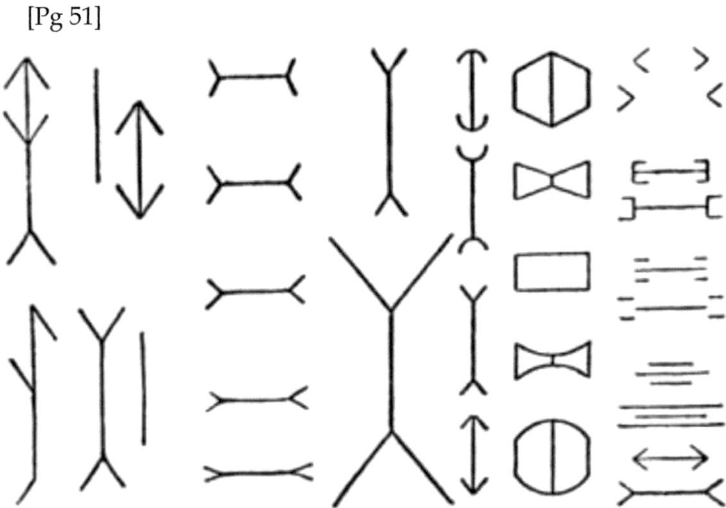

Compare perpendicular and horizontal lines: The angles
and curves which enclose them change their relative equality.

ILLUSION EFFECT AND EXPRESSION IN THE USE OF LINES

107. We very often notice a room which has been carefully carried out but is utterly lacking in charm. The color seems right, and, considered in detail, the furniture and the furnishings are appropriate, but the room lacks effectiveness.

It is uninteresting.

It is like a doll face that is, perhaps, perfect in detail, but utterly devoid of expression.

The artist who paints a portrait is a failure without the ability to give expression: hence in [Pg 52] architecture the acute-angled spires or arched roofs have the same expression that the "long face" carries.

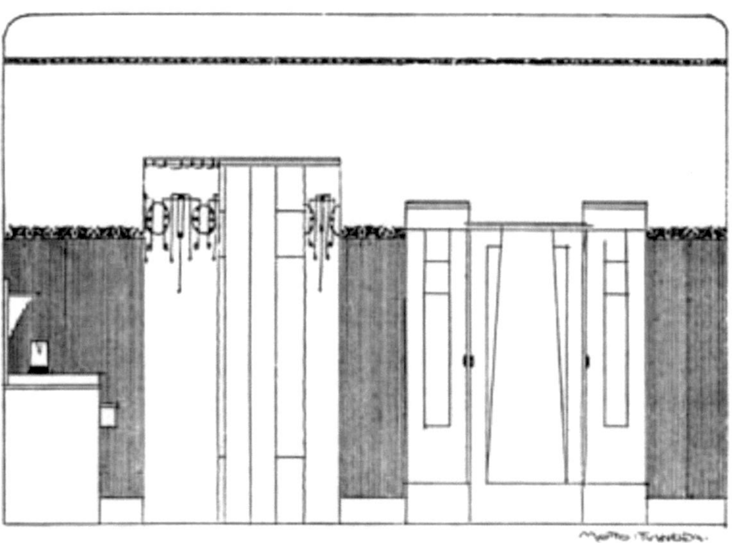

If we smile, the mouth curves upward; if we grieve, the lines turn downward.

108. In festival decorations, joy is expressed by loops, curves and festoons.

109. In serious decorations (libraries, studies, church or office work) straight lines are used; curtains are gathered in plaits so that the sags and drapes are all out of them; they are drawn. It is the same when we say of a person: "He looks serious, his face is drawn; it is full of lines."

110. The observation, "a broad smile on his face," [Pg 53] means literally just that; the lines extend outward and upward, giving an expression of breadth and joy to the countenance.

ILLUSION

111. A doorway looks wider that has at the top a drapery which crosses in one complete curved sweep. A side-wall is larger apparently if along the frieze line long, wide loops or festoons are arranged. The same wall is more contracted and higher if treated in arrow-point forms of design.

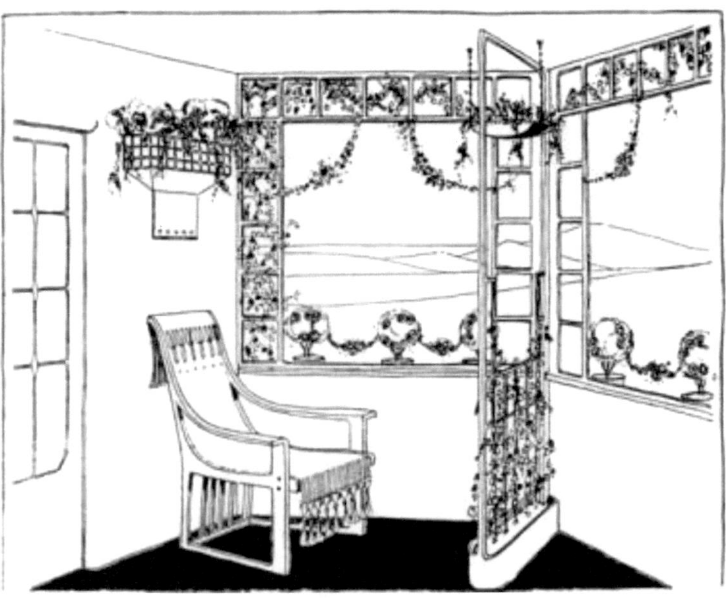

The decorator should study these matters of [Pg 54] illusion, for they are vital to the success of his labor. (See ¶ 116.)

112. Perpendicular lines contract the wall space and extend the apparent height of a room; horizontal lines shorten the apparent height of the ceiling and lengthen the width of the room. (See exceptions, ¶ 119.)

These straight lines may be used where extremes are needed. (See pages 61 and 63.)

A short doorway, for instance, looks higher where the portière is hung in straight folds; so also with a cottage window.

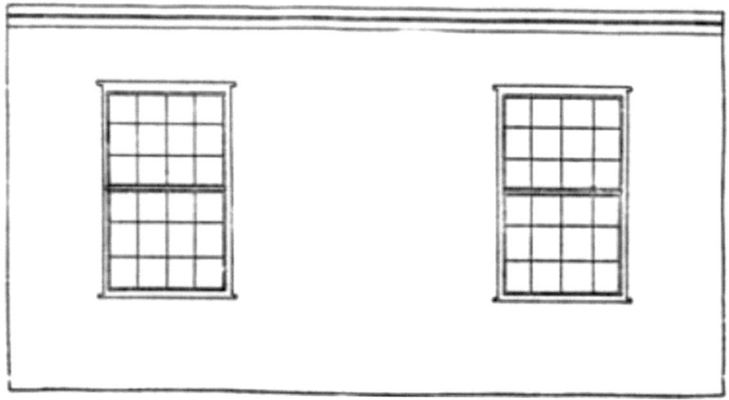

113. Every decorator who handles fabrics, every cabinetmaker who lays out the woodwork of a room, every stained glass window maker, should appreciate one fact: A line which is finished at the top or [Pg 55] bottom, or both, with acute angles appears longer than the line that is finished top and bottom with an obtuse or right angle. It is the same with the finish of a wall frieze.

If the wall frieze ends abruptly (Illustration A on page 57), it is foreshortened; if it is finished by angles (Illustration B), the height of the room is apparently greater. (See the illustration on page 51.)

114. It is the same way with curves; given two lines of equal length and enclose one with convex and the other with concave curves, and the line enclosed convex will appear longer.

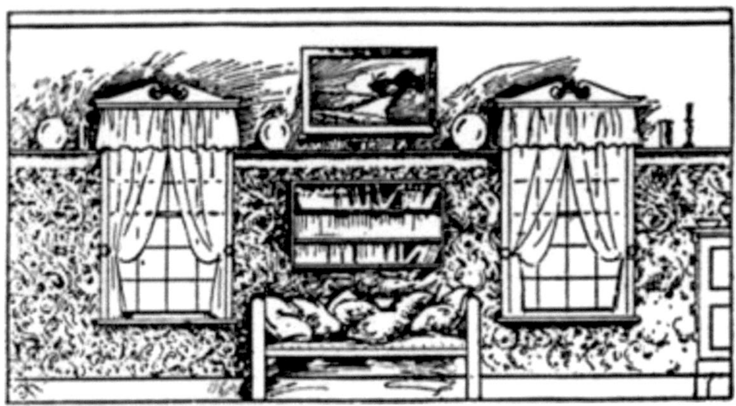

Treated for Broken Heights.

[Pg 56]

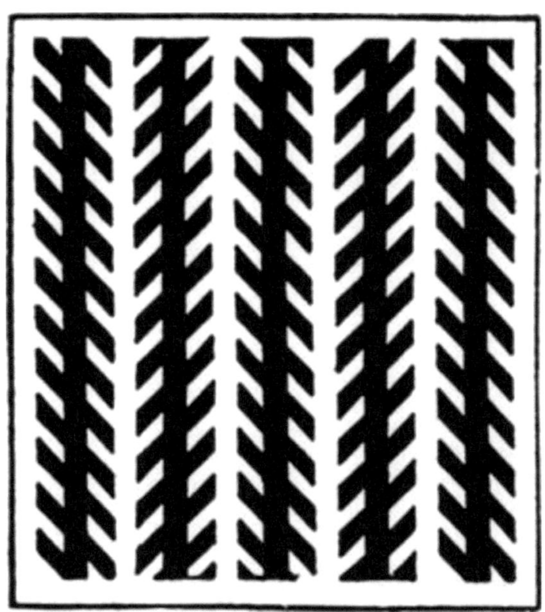

115. In dress a collar brought down to an acute angle in the front of the waist gives height effect, whereas a perfectly straight collar around the neck reduces the apparent height and gives width effect.

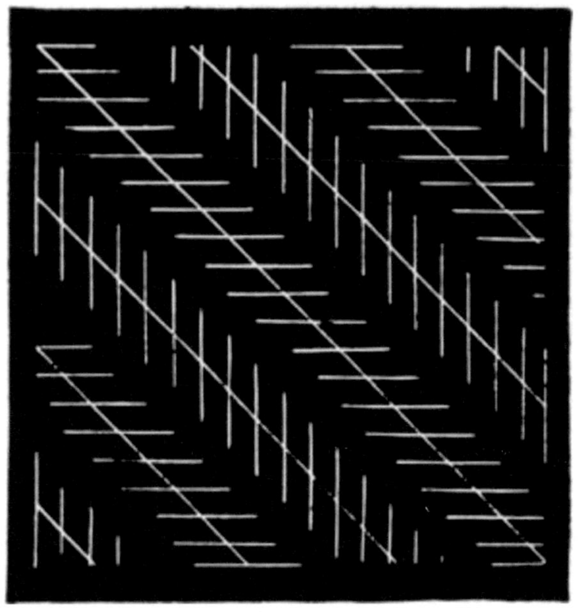

116. The use of arches should be studied. A space that is arched looks wider than it actually is, for the eye unconsciously follows the lines of the arch, and a distance or width effect is the result. The same space treated with a straight line is quickly bridged. The same space treated with lines that come to an angle looks narrower, for the reason that the eye becomes focused by the apex of the angle, and a height effect, not a breadth effect, is the result. (See page 57.)

117. This illusion is best shown in the illustrations of the parallel lines that are crossed diagonally, with the result that the lines no longer look parallel because of the angles. Nevertheless, they are parallel, and the lines running diagonally at the bottom of this page are also parallel.

We present two practical illustrations of illusion in the use of lines. (See ¶ 112.) They represent the side-walls of two rooms of the same dimensions, but showing apparently different proportions, the perpendicular lines making the side-wall look higher and the horizontal lines making the side-wall look lower. (See page 59.)

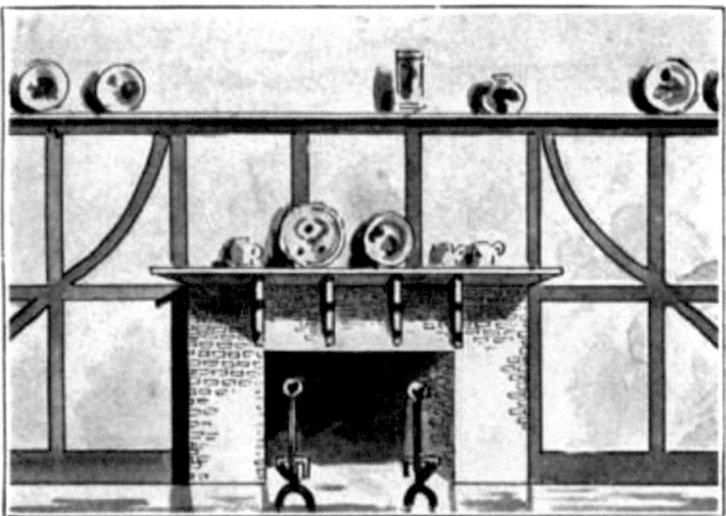

Illustration A.

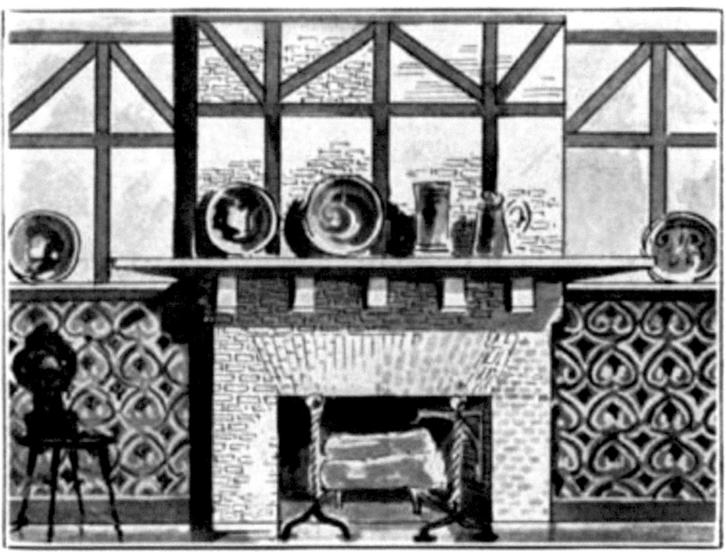

Illustration B. (See ¶ 113.)

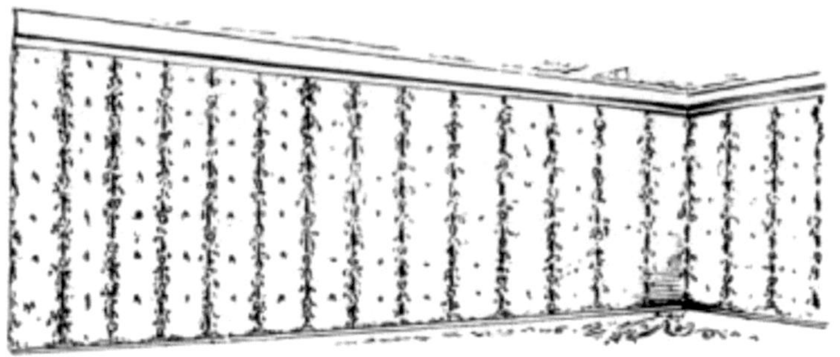

The length of the wall space is shortened, moreover, by the perpendicular lines and lengthened by the horizontal lines.

118. No period expresses more clearly the joy of curves as opposed to the severity of straight lines than that voluptuous period of Louis XV known as Rococo. It was a profligate era, an era of pleasure, and the appended illustration of part of a frieze is in no way exaggerated, but a true example of a common expression. (See page 60.)

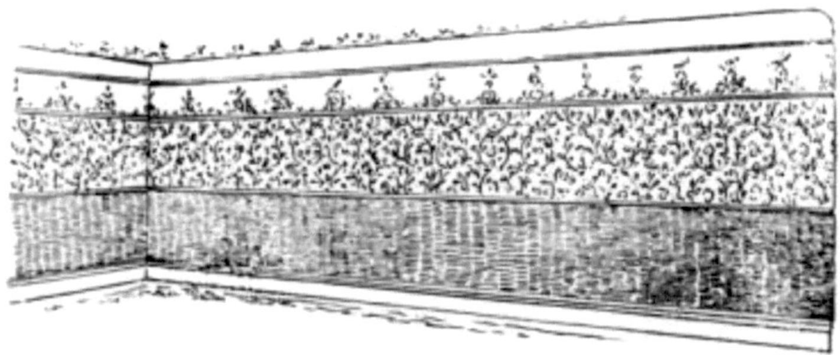

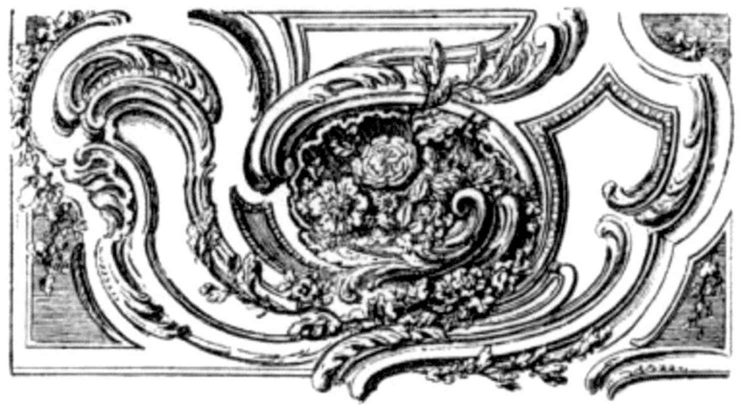

119. Distinct perpendicular lines give height effect, but they also narrow the apparent width of a wall space. It is best to have such line effects indistinct unless they appear as in the illustration on page 63, where they are intended to reduce the breadth effect of the pattern and neutralize a squat tendency.

Indistinct perpendiculars give height effect, and do not reduce the wall width.

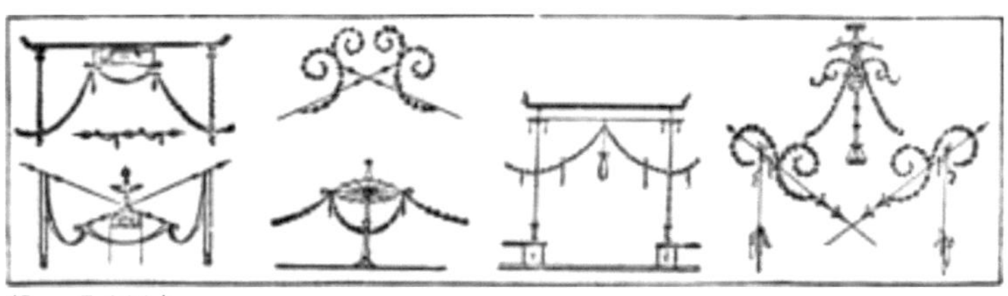

(See ¶ 111.)

[Pg 61]

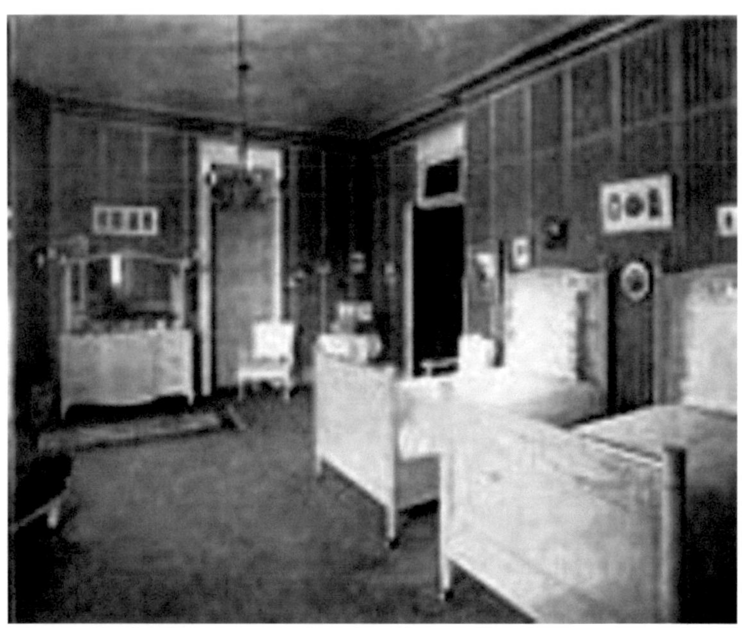

Perpendicular lines, giving height effect.

[Pg 63]

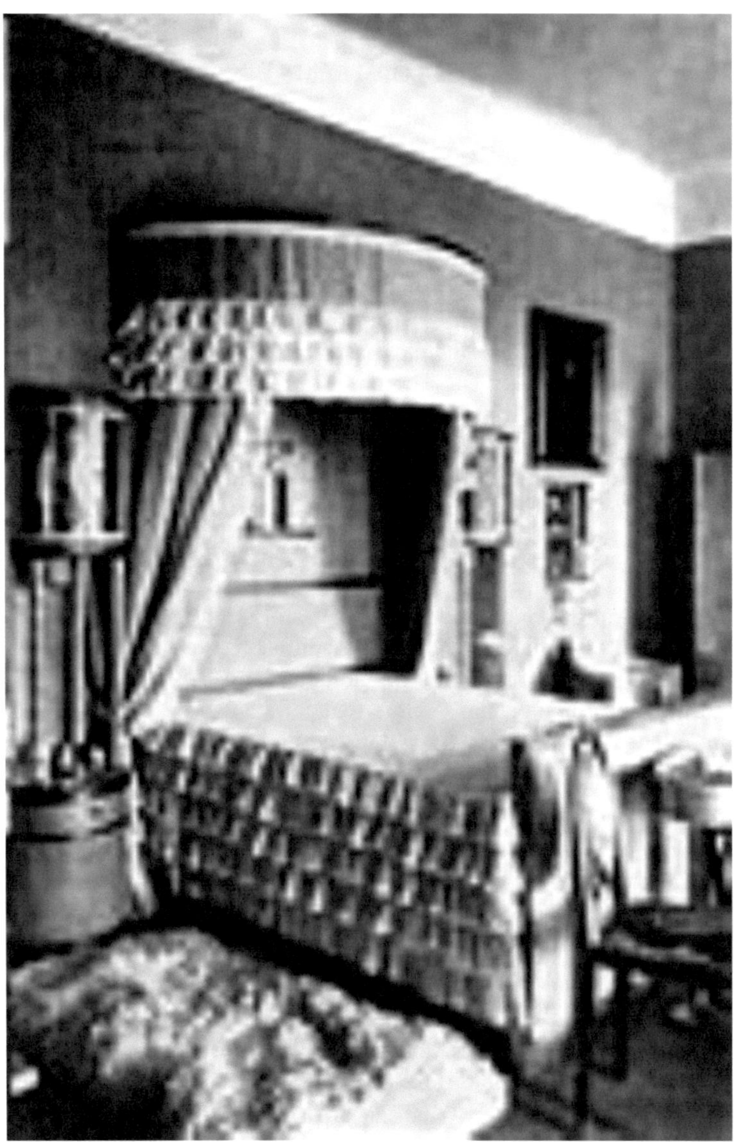

Perpendicular lines, giving height effect.

COLOR TERMS

120. In the study of color and its application authorities differ so materially that it is not only impossible to reconcile their theories, but the different terms used to express color thought create inextricable confusion.

121. One authority fixes the neutrals as being black, gray and white; another regards them as those hues or tones which lack definite color, like quaternaries. Authorities differ, moreover, upon even the fundamental principles. Chevreuil selects red, yellow and blue as the primaries; Dr. Thomas Young selects red, green and violet. Helmholtz selects carmine, pale green and blue-violet; Maxwell scarlet red, emerald green and blue-violet; Professor Rood agrees with Maxwell; Professor Church, of the Royal Academy of Arts, London, regards the primaries as red, green and blue; George Hurst, the English authority, fixes upon red, yellow and blue, the Brewsterian theory.

122. One must remember always in studying color that we are treating with the material, not with the illusion. We are dealing with pigments, not with prismatic phenomena, and it must be obvious that the only three primary colors that can be used in a way to produce all other colors are red, yellow and blue.

123. Whatever may be the spectrum theories of Sir Isaac Newton, Young or Helmholtz, for practical reasons we prefer to follow an authority as eminent as Chevreuil, for years the head of the National Gobelin Works of France, and a man experienced in the [Pg 66] practice as well as the theory of color. Any effort to fix the character of color and describe it by periods and epochs will always prove unsatisfactory, for the reason that terms and expressions have changed with every period since the Egyptian, 4000 B.C.

124. We think we know purple until we discover that the purple of royalty, the ermine and purple, the purple of the cardinals' robes, frequently approximated what we now call carmine. Royal purple and Venetian blue are mere trade terms. Practical men in the purchase of things decorative soon discover that color terms convey only individual impressions and no distinctive qualities that may be

relied upon; so that any effort to fix the color value by periods would be futile. We may assume that in the age of oak, mahogany, white and gold or walnut furniture, the fabric and wall colors harmonized with the wood colors, and to that degree we may fix the period character of color. The moment that the tone of the woodwork or the light conditions varied, color character varied also.

125. We must also bear well in mind that colors which have come down to us as examples of ancient times have been subjected to the changing influences of centuries, and have faded and altered. The colors on the walls of the historic rooms of European palaces have greatly altered. The flat reds and the deadish blues of the Pompeiian frescoes have been altered by chemical action during the 1,850 years' burial under the lava of Vesuvius. We are not justified in judging [Pg 67] of the colors of A.D. 79 by the restoration-examples in 1900. Hence the mere expressions Pompeiian red, Pompeiian blue, can convey no definite, positive meaning.

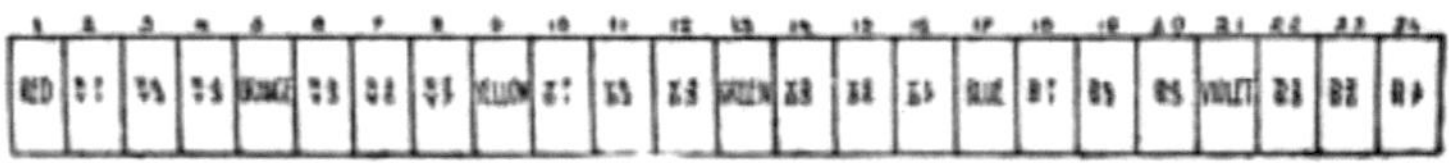

Fig. 1.

COLOR VOCABULARY

126. In music, a tone which is formed by a certain number of vibrations per second is the same the world over, and each and every tone has a name; but in color no such standards exist. People have attempted to formulate a system by denominating the primary colors, red, yellow and blue, respectively as R, Y and B, and the combinations of these colors as combinations of letters. For example, red, with varying degrees of yellow added, is denominated by the letters R R O, or R O R, or O O R. This system tends to confusion, and is inadequate to express tints and shades. Various other systems have been devised. Color charts have been made, and in each system arbitrary names have been assigned, so that each color may be known by one of several names. The difficulty of insuring accuracy under these circumstances becomes very evident.

127. In discussing color combinations, one is usually confused because the subject is not a tangible expression that can be grasped like the sound of a note [Pg 68] in music. With color charts, every maker has a standard of his own and the term "red" may mean anything within a wide range; a yellow-red or a blue-red, the yellow-red perhaps being cherry, the blue-red perhaps being carmine. An appreciation of the Harmonies of Contrast or Harmonies of Analogy or Relationship is accompanied by great confusion because of this lack of standardization.

128. There is only one true standard of color, and that is the standard as shown in the prism, and expressed by the spectrum. It is within the province of any man to determine the proper relationship of color if he starts with the chart we here present. We fix definitely the three primary and the three secondary colors, the primaries, red, yellow and blue, being those indicated by the heavy black lines; the secondaries, orange, green and violet, being indicated by the broad stipple lines.

All other lines are the tertiary or quaternary colors.

If we have clearly in our minds the appearance of the normal red and yellow, and clearly in our minds the orange that is made up by combining the two, we ought to be able to fix in our imagination the colors that come midway between the red and the orange, or the colors that come nearer the red or nearer the orange. Let us assume we are to select colors in the harmony of *contrast*. Take a ruler and lay across the chart and the contrasting colors are always opposite; the direct contrast of red is green because green is [Pg 69] composed of the other two primary colors, yellow and blue; the contrast of blue is orange because orange is a combination of the other two primaries, yellow and red; the contrast of yellow is violet, a combination of blue and red.

Now, to determine the niceties of distinction, let us take a red that is a little off shade, a little yellowish; one must determine in the mind's eye about how much yellow there is in it and, to determine the true contrast, carry your line across from the point which you think is represented by the yellowish and you find that it is green with a little blue added, or bluish-green.

129. One must also determine the scale of color. The parallel circular lines on the chart designate four scales, or four grades, of each color, growing lighter by adding white, to the center; as you add more and more white the tint becomes more and more light. In determining contrast, be careful to stick to your scale. Contrasts, to be in harmony, must be colors of the same scale.

130. Harmony of analogy or relationship is clearly expressed in the chart. The family relations of red are the things which go with red. We may have a harmony of analogy in violet which includes the relations of red and blue. We must not attempt to carry the family relationship too far. There is a wide range of variety in these combinations of analogy because they may include not only all scales of each color from the darkest tones to the lightest tints but they include tertiaries and quaternaries.

[Pg 70] Each man must establish his own standard, and by establishing it he forms unconsciously a very comprehensive understanding of color. It has never been possible to print a true colored chart because no two copies of the sheet off the press would be alike. A little more ink or a little less ink, or a little lighter or a little heavier impression, changes the values.

The chart illustrates contrasts of all of the primaries and secondary colors and the broken colors or hues. In the same way the tertiary or quaternary colors may be arranged, but for convenience we show the contrasts as follows:

Russet:
Tertiary,
32 parts Red, 16 parts Yellow, 16 parts Blue
31 parts Red, 16 parts Yellow, 17 parts Blue
30 parts Red, 16 parts Yellow, 18 parts Blue
29 parts Red, 16 parts Yellow, 19 parts Blue
28 parts Red, 16 parts Yellow, 20 parts Blue
27 parts Red, 16 parts Yellow, 21 parts Blue
26 parts Red, 16 parts Yellow, 22 parts Blue
25 parts Red, 16 parts Yellow, 23 parts Blue
Slate:
Tertiary,
32 parts Blue, 16 parts Red, 16 parts Yellow

31 parts Blue, 16 parts Red, 17 parts Yellow
30 parts Blue, 16 parts Red, 18 parts Yellow
29 parts Blue, 16 parts Red, 19 parts Yellow
28 parts Blue, 16 parts Red, 20 parts Yellow
27 parts Blue, 16 parts Red, 21 parts Yellow
26 parts Blue, 16 parts Red, 22 parts Yellow
25 parts Blue, 16 parts Red, 23 parts Yellow
Citrine:

Tertiary,

32 parts Yellow, 16 parts Blue, 16 parts Red
31 parts Yellow, 16 parts Blue, 17 parts Red
30 parts Yellow, 16 parts Blue, 18 parts Red
29 parts Yellow, 16 parts Blue, 19 parts Red
28 parts Yellow, 16 parts Blue, 20 parts Red
27 parts Yellow, 16 parts Blue, 21 parts Red
26 parts Yellow, 16 parts Blue, 22 parts Red
25 parts Yellow, 16 parts Blue, 23 parts Red
Sage:

Quaternary,

24 parts Blue, 16 parts Red, 24 parts Yellow
25 parts Yellow, 23 parts Blue, 16 parts Red
26 parts Yellow, 22 parts Blue, 16 parts Red
27 parts Yellow, 21 parts Blue, 16 parts Red
28 parts Yellow, 20 parts Blue, 16 parts Red
29 parts Yellow, 19 parts Blue, 16 parts Red
30 parts Yellow, 18 parts Blue, 16 parts Red
31 parts Yellow, 17 parts Blue, 16 parts Red
Buff:

Quaternary,

24 parts Yellow, 16 parts Blue, 24 parts Red
25 parts Red, 23 parts Yellow, 16 parts Blue
26 parts Red, 22 parts Yellow, 16 parts Blue
27 parts Red, 21 parts Yellow, 16 parts Blue
28 parts Red, 20 parts Yellow, 16 parts Blue
29 parts Red, 19 parts Yellow, 16 parts Blue
30 parts Red, 18 parts Yellow, 16 parts Blue
31 parts Red, 17 parts Yellow, 16 parts Blue
Plum:

Quaternary,

24 parts Red, 16 parts Yellow, 24 parts Blue
25 parts Blue, 23 parts Red, 16 parts Yellow
26 parts Blue, 22 parts Red, 16 parts Yellow
27 parts Blue, 21 parts Red, 16 parts Yellow
28 parts Blue, 20 parts Red, 16 parts Yellow
29 parts Blue, 19 parts Red, 16 parts Yellow
30 parts Blue, 18 parts Red, 16 parts Yellow
31 parts Blue, 17 parts Red, 16 parts Yellow

[Pg 73]

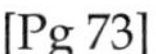

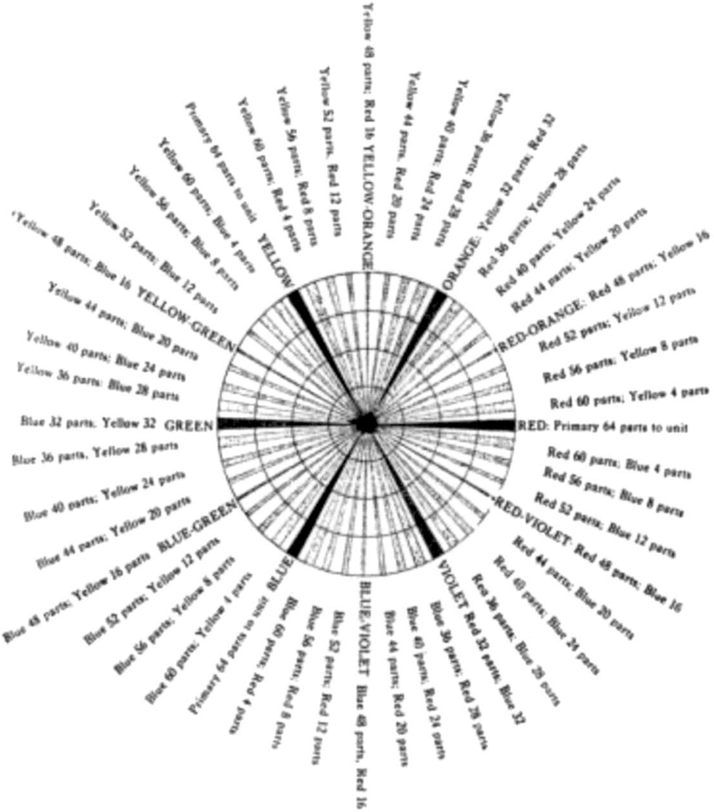

[Pg 74] 131. One who attempts to make color compositions with no more reliable guide than taste can expect to accomplish no more than he who in music possesses a good ear but no musical training.

132. The note of discord in color is best avoided by an infallible guide, as the discord in music is best avoided by thorough training in the law of harmony. The color chart on page 73 has been so arranged that each of the shades is in exact harmony with the shade directly opposite.

133. For example, to ascertain the color that is in harmony with the shade denominated Red-Orange, it is necessary simply to lay a ruler across the diagram to find the corresponding harmony, which is Blue-Green.

134. We know that the primary colors are red, yellow and blue, and that the combination of any two of these gives a secondary color. The secondary color is the complement of the remaining third color; thus yellow and blue form green, and green is the complement or contrasting harmony of red. Red and yellow form orange, and orange is the complement of blue. Blue and red form violet, and violet is the complement of yellow. These are facts we all know. Now, if red is the complement or contrasting harmony of green, and yellow contrasts with violet, then red with one, two or three degrees of yellow added will contrast with green with one, two or three degrees of blue added.

Assume, for example, that a decorator dealing with a red side-wall wishes upholsterings in the correct [Pg 75] shade of green. He knows he has a red wall, he knows also that he wishes to use some shade of green, but without some fixed standard it is impossible for him to do more than approximate the correct shade of green to use. If, however, he could compare the red of his wall with his color chart and determine exactly which of the many shades of red, or which of the many yellow reds, or blue reds, the wall is toned in, it is a simple process to ascertain the exact green harmonizing with this red.

The second great use of the color chart is then an infallible guide to color harmony, whether analagous or contrasting.

This line shows the colors of the normal scale running from Red (R) to Yellow (Y) to Blue (B) to Red (R).

This line and all below it show the same primary and secondary colors lightened by added white.

A color is indicated by the intersection lines perpendicular and horizontal.

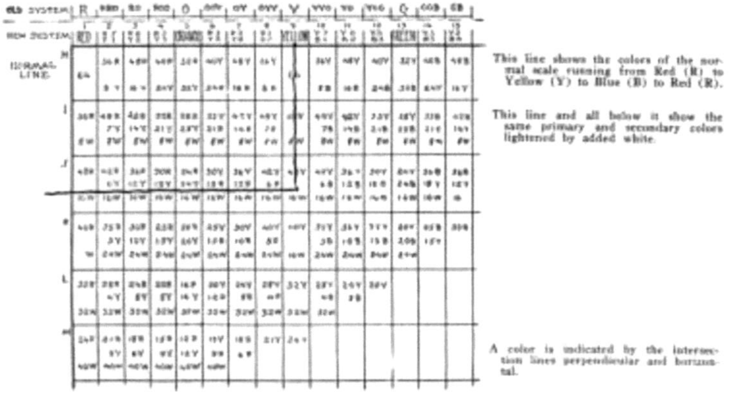

(TN: Click on image for large scale version.)

ARTIFICIAL LIGHTING

135. In considering artificial light, we will avoid all efforts to analyze the different forms of energy, magnetic energy, electric energy, heat energy, mechanical momentum, radiating energy, and deal with result rather than with cause and effect. It will be sufficient to state as the deduction of the scientist that certain waves or vibrations which affect the fibers of the optic nerve are transmitted by the brain into color. (¶ 3.) Self-luminous bodies are bodies which produce light. Illuminated bodies shine by borrowed light, and are distinguished by the different amounts and quantities of light which they reflect. A dense cloud which appears nearly black when between the observer's eye and the sun, owing to the degree of density with which it intercepts the light, may become brilliantly white when the sun's rays fall upon its constituent particles, for the light which cannot penetrate the cloud is continually reflected to and from the surface of its minute parts. Thus it happens that the lower part of a cloud seen against a background of dark mountain may appear white, while the upper part may appear dull gray. In the alteration of reflection we [Pg 78] have an alteration of color. A stick of sealing wax will show in some positions white reflected

light, while in other positions we see only the red. A polished plane furnishes one kind of reflection, a piece of chalk another.

136. The decorator has for years past been disposed to defer to the illuminating engineer in the artificial lighting of a home. But while the technical man or engineer may have a knowledge of power and energy, he has not studied the decorative value of lighting. His problem has been economic rather than psychologic. The illuminating engineer cannot be expected to appreciate fully the harmonies of color in decoration.

137. It is the decorator's province to consider not only the power of light in the furnishing of a house, but the character of the light — not only its color influence, but the structural character of its introduction, as affecting these furnishings. It is beyond his province to determine whether carbon should be replaced by tantalum, osmium or tungsten to get higher efficiency, but he must understand the effects of these lights and prescribe accordingly.

ABSORPTION AND REFLECTION

138. The architect who designates the number and location of outlets for the lighting sources, and specifies the candle-power of the lamps, knows nothing of the ultimate decoration of the house. Very often the specifications are finished before the color scheme has been decided upon, and as a result the degree of [Pg 79] illumination either falls short of what is needed in case of dark-colored interiors, or proves excessive with light-tinted rooms. The architect works from one point, economy, the decorator from another, æsthetic; while the householder, the consumer who pays the illuminating bills, cannot comprehend why his lighting bills increase as his taste for luminous or dark-colored furnishings is gratified. Many houses are left in the white plaster for a year or more until the plaster settles. In this condition a small unit of light is sufficient, but when the decorator completes his work, adding fabrics and wallpapers which absorb and diminish the light, the householder, unaware of the cause, notices a material increase in his bills for illumination. These facts must be understood to be remedied, and it remains for the illuminating engineer to determine by direct experiment the value of any light as it affects and influences color, as well

as the value of color as it affects light. It may be assumed without danger that the softest light is that of the candle, but we are not living in the candle age, and have to deal with either gas or electricity as the main illuminating agents.

139. We have to consider the mercury arc light, the yellow flame carbon, the white magnetite and titanium arc—all of high efficiency, giving orange yellow in the flame-carbon to yellow and yellow white in the acetyline of the tungsten filaments. Then we have the greenish yellow of the Welsbach mantle, the bluish green of the mercury arc, the yellowish white [Pg 80] of the carbon arc, as well as the clear white of the titanium arc.

140. The subject may be divided into three heads: Quality, or approximation to natural light. Quantity, as demanded by reflection or absorption. Installation, diffusion or mechanical distribution.

141. Normal light is the light of general diffusion in daylight, and when we can find an artificial light that has the character of natural light we will have what is obviously the best illuminant for the home. Bear in mind that natural light as it appears out of doors is materially altered when indoors by the presence of different planes and angles, which cast and receive various depths of shadow; the quality required is that which will provide illumination without glare. The sun's rays are softened and mellowed by the depth of air through which they pass, and it is this mellowness that is the chief requisite in illumination.

Good decorative illumination does not mean illumination that reveals every hidden corner of a room. We need shadows to betray form, relieve monotony and give depth to the *ensemble*. If in an illuminated area light is of a uniform intensity, we have a bad effect. The variation of tone in a fabric is due to the light reaching it from a given point. Differences in intensity make shadows and tones.

142. The illuminating engineer treats the home as he treats a public hall. He ignores the individuality of the room; the ball-room and the sickroom are lighted [Pg 81] alike. He does not always consider the diminished force of light as it passes through a refracting surface, for it must be borne in mind that any method of indirect lighting by refraction is apt to cause a loss of volume. The use of various kinds of globes or lamp shades must all be considered. A light-

colored wall reflects illumination, a dark-colored wall absorbs it; hence the amount of illumination is increased or diminished by the color of the walls.

LIGHT EFFECT ON COLOR

143. To illuminate a city, with the dull grim environment of streets and houses, a soft yellow glow will give warmth and tone; the greenish yellow of the Welsbach or the blue green of the mercury arc may even be desirable, but the same green or violet rays are ghastly in a house, and should never be permitted.

144. The warm glow of the yellow light, while pleasing to the complexion, is, however, objectionable as disturbing the color composition of dress or furnishings. A gaslight sends a yellow glow over all that it reaches, and has the same effect as the introduction of yellow into every color tint in the room. The walls that are red take on a scarlet hue; the scarlet ones are yellowed to orange; the blues become greenish.

145. In order that the decorator may more readily grasp the subject, we have arranged a table showing the color changes effected by rays of yellow, blue, green and violet:

[Pg 82]

Orange rays falling on white make it appear orange.
   " " red it appears reddish-orange.
   " " orange it appears deeper orange.
   " " yellow it appears orange-yellow.
   " " green it appears dark yellow-green.
   " " blue it appears dark reddish-gray.
   " " violet it appears dark purplish-gray.
   " " black it appears brownish-black.
Yellow rays falling on white make it appear yellow.
   " " red make it appear orange-brown.
   " " orange make it appear orange-yellow.
   " " yellow make it appear deeper yellow.
   " " green make it appear yellowish-green.
   " " blue make it appear slaty-gray.

" " violet make it appear purplish-gray.
" " black make it appear olive-black.
Green rays falling on white make it appear green.
" " red make it appear yellowish-brown.
" " orange make it appear grayish-leaf-green.
" " yellow make it appear yellowish-green.
" " green make it appear deeper green.
" " blue make it appear bluish-green.
" " violet make it appear bluish-gray.
" " black make it appear dark greenish-gray.
Blue rays falling on white make it appear blue.
" " red make it appear purple.
" " orange make it appear plum-brown.
" " yellow make it appear yellowish-gray.
" " green make it appear bluish-green.
" " blue make it appear deeper blue.
" " violet make it appear bluer.
" " black make it appear bluish-black.
Violet rays falling on white make it appear violet.
" " red make it appear purple.
" " orange make it appear reddish-gray.
" " yellow make it appear purplish-gray.
" " green make it appear bluish-gray.
" " blue make it appear bluish-violet.
" " violet make it appear deeper violet.
" " black make it appear violet-black.

[Pg 83] 146. The pale tints of electric lights, which make every face in a room look ghastly, will affect quite as disastrously every soft color in the furnishings. In ordinary gaslight a pair of white gloves looks yellow, and we have seen Welsbach lamps which threw out a violet-blue illumination, depressing in the extreme. Under a yellow glow, blues, greens, violets and purples are greatly changed. Under a violet glow, yellows and greens are ruined. To see all colors in about the same value that they possess by daylight one must have a light in which no color tone is apparent.

The question as to the disposition and intensity of the lights is of vital importance, and must be considered with the requirements of each particular room in mind.

147. For the drawing-room and reception-room it is desirable that all parts of the room be evenly lighted, without a pronounced glare in any particular part of the room. One of the most effective ways of accomplishing this is by distributing the lights around the room, either on the ceiling, in the cove or above a wide molding, so that the ceiling acts as a reflecting agent, and distributes an even tone of light to all parts.

ILLUMINATION

148. For the dining-room and living-room a different plan must be used, because of the different requirements. The table is usually in such rooms the chief feature of the furnishings, and it is customary to focus upon it the main body of light. While this is [Pg 84] obviously necessary, the surroundings must not be ignored; neither is it possible to raise the center light to such a height that its radiation may reach all parts of the room, because in so doing the light reaches the eye at an extremely unpleasant angle. The drop fixture should be low enough to effectively light all parts of the table, while at the same time its shade should screen the light from the eyes of the room's occupants. To illuminate the surrounding parts of the room other lights should be distributed where they will most effectively supply what further illumination is required.

149. For the bedroom or boudoir the location of the lights should also be subordinated to the purposes of the room, and in addition to providing sufficient illumination to the entire area, special illumination should be provided for the mirrors and the dressing-table. The lights for the mirrors should be planned to illuminate the person and not the image.

150. For large reception-rooms in hotels and public institutions the plan is frequently adopted of having all light provided by small table lamps with opalescent shades. These provide a medium glow throughout the entire room that is pleasing, and avoid entirely the garishness usually associated with such rooms. One of the mistakes of the day is the use of high-power lights, which are so intense that they require to be screened or shaded, involving waste of light and concentrating an unnecessary amount of illumination upon a narrow sphere.

REFLECTIVE POWER OF COLOR

The following table will give an idea of the percentage of light reflected from ordinary wall-hangings and papers:

	Per Cent. Reflection
White blotting-paper	.82
White cartridge-paper	.80
Ordinary foolscap	.70
Ordinary newspaper	.50 to .70
Chrome yellow paper	.62
Orange paper	.50
Yellow wall-paper	.40
Yellow painted wall (clean)	.40
Tracing cloth, pale blue	.35
Light pink paper	.36
Blue paper	.25
Emerald green	.18
Dark brown paper	.13
Vermilion paper	.12
Blue green paper	.12
Cobalt blue paper	.12
Black paper	0.5
Deep chocolate paper	0.4
French ultramarine blue paper	3.5
Black cloth	1.2
Black velvet	0.4

151. It is very difficult to select practical artificial illuminants, because of the various color properties possessed by each. A Welsbach mantle, which gives a greenish tint, is pretty sure to alter the character of any color other than green. Incandescent electric light, as well as ordinary gaslight, contains a yellow tint.

[Pg 86]

THE COLOR OF ARTIFICIAL LIGHTS

152. In planning or matching colors for a room, it is best to consider the purpose for which the room is to be used, and match the colors under the same light conditions that will prevail in the finished room.

Deep, full colors are less affected by the shadings in artificial illuminants than lighter tones of the same color.

Illuminant.	Color.
Sun (high in sky)	White.
Sun (near horizon)	Orange red.
Sky light	Bluish white.
Electric arc (short)	White.
Electric arc (long)	Bluish white to violet.
Nernst lamp	White.
Incandescent (normal)	Yellow-white.
Incandescent (below voltage)	Orange to orange-red.
Acetyline flame	Nearly white.
Welsbach light	Greenish white.
Gaslight (Siemens burner)	Nearly white, faint yellow tinge.
Gaslight (ordinary)	Yellowish white to pale orange.
Kerosene lamp	Yellowish white to pale orange.
Candle	Orange yellow.

ARTIFICIAL LIGHT APPLICATION

153. The introduction of light by the medium of a wire, which may be carried to any point in a room, encourages so many possibilities for comfort and effect that it behooves us to forget traditional customs which were established during the gaslight period. The introduction of gaslight through tubes was a rather complex problem, and the carrying of the pipes into the room through a main chandelier was the most [Pg 87] advisable constructive form. But we have no need for such cumbersome fixtures in this day of wiring.

A mere cord takes the place of an inch pipe. Modern German and Austrian lighting fixtures frequently are mere pendants, with the cord frankly in evidence. In this way the lights may be placed wherever needed — at the head of the lounge, so one may read more clearly by it; close by the piano; over the tea-table. In fact, supplementary lights to the general illumination are a convenience that the decorator should consider.

154. The lighting of a house is a matter so dependent upon æsthetic conditions that it is never within the scope of the electrician. It is a problem for a decorator alone to solve. Intense and glaring lights of unusual power must be avoided. Luminants of low intrinsic brilliancy are preferable.

155. The floor is the least important surface for illumination, and has no reflecting power of value. The walls vary in value according to their color and surface. With lights radiating upward, however, the ceiling possesses definite power, and should be considered.

156. Dark colors absorb light, while white and light colors reflect, and this must always be remembered; for upon the character of the decorations and furnishings of various rooms the quantity as well as the quality of light has serious influence.

POWER NECESSARY

157. While the list which we give herewith is [Pg 88] based largely upon area, it may be taken as a basis of calculation for lighting equipment.

It is estimated that 300 square feet of a hallway requires four sixteen-candlepower, or eight eight-candlepower units.

In a room 20 x 20 feet, with furnishings of mahogany and green, broken up by bookcases and other furniture producing heavy shadows, it is estimated that twelve eight-candlepower lights are sufficient if worked into the frieze, and that a reading lamp of not less than thirty-two-candlepower be used as a drop light.

Assuming a room is 15 x 15 feet, and furnished in light tones, four eight-candlepower lamps are ample.

A living-room 20 x 25 feet, in light tones of color, requires two thirty-two-candlepower lights, centrally located, and about twelve eight-candlepower lights. This should provide brilliant illumination.

A room 15 x 20 feet, in dark wood and hangings, needs eight eight-candlepower reflector lamps, backed up by six more eight-candlepower lamps.

Bedrooms 15 x 15 feet in size, where they are not furnished in deep colors, should be equipped with two sixteen-candlepower lights.

COLOR CONTROL

158. Mechanical lighting is so easily undertaken that it predisposes one to extravagance. Properly applied, artificial light adds materially to the charm of a room, but with illumination secured by the mere twist of the wrist one is prone to ignore the value of shadows and kill the beauty of light and shade by throwing [Pg 89] illumination into the remotest corners. The danger to good decoration is not only in overlighting, but in overdecorating, and commercialism naturally encourages this tendency. The floor is frequently best treated if not entirely covered with a one-pattern treatment; the walls are frequently most pleasing if done in several papers instead of one. The most effective room is the one lighted in various degrees of strength, and while the decorator unconsciously follows this idea and avoids superabundance of pattern by using panels, friezes and wainscotings, we believe that each and every section or part of a

room should be treated separately, observing, of course, a consistent spirit of design, preserving the period style and the general color effect; we would vary the actual shade of coloring and the size of pattern according to the dimensions of the wall space it occupies. The large patterns and the strong colorings which may be appropriate to an exposed wall are all out of proportion in narrow or darkened confines. Dark and deep recesses should obviously be treated differently to advanced or conspicuous spaces.

159. At a recent meeting of the Illuminating Engineering Society, D. McFarlan Moore made the following observations: "A few years ago there was practically no way of changing the colors of the various forms of lamps, that is, the candle had its color perforce; such a thing as modifying it was not dreamed of. The oil lamp had its color; the open burner gas flame its color, the incandescent lamp its color, and the [Pg 90] arc lamp its color. At the present time there are only two ways widely in use of varying the color; that is, if a person wishes to have a light of a different color, there are two main ways of getting it. One way is to get another light source, and the other way is to use a diffusion globe of some kind, which in any instance is extremely unscientific and inefficient. Some of the most recent advances in this line are connected with the flaming arc lamp. There we have an instance where the first step, at least, was taken toward scientifically controlling the color value. I refer to placing different chemicals in the carbon and thereby obtaining a color which can, to a very great extent, be determined previously. But still it by no means can be said that by means of the flaming arc lamp the color factor is under perfect control. However, it is possible now to have the color value under perfect control, and this is obtained by utilizing a vacuum tube, and by changing the various gases used in the tube to change the color. This has many advantages, and from a scientific standpoint it cannot be criticised, as can the other methods which have been used. For example, if you use a properly regulated vacuum tube and feed it with air only, a pink light results; if you feed it with nitrogen a yellow light results, and such a light can be used for a great many purposes; in fact its range of usefulness so far as the color is concerned, is about the same as that of the ordinary incandescent lamp, and therefore can be used by florists or by clothing merchants, and the distortion is

not any worse than [Pg 91] that of the ordinary incandescent lamp. However, it is not by any means claimed that when a tube is fed nitrogen, that the color is at all near daylight; it is simply a color which appears about the same as that produced by the ordinary incandescent lamp. Due to the enormous radiating surfaces of the tube, the color in day time looks considerably redder than that of the incandescent lamp because the lamp is extremely small as compared with the tube. When such a tube is fed with carbon dioxide at a definite pressure, and at a definite intensity, a light is obtained that undoubtedly is closer to average daylight color values than any light which has ever been produced before, and we can almost say that it is entirely satisfactory. For instance, experts in matching colors in the largest dye works of this country, men who have tried all other forms of light, and found them not at all suitable for their uses, have matched their colors under a vacuum tube supplied with carbon dioxide and have found after months of practical use that they could not detect any difference between most delicate lavender shades, when they are matched at night time under the tube and in day time by daylight, not direct sunlight."

DRESS AND COMPLEXION

160. The nerves of the eye, exhilarated by any pronounced color, unconsciously observe the complement of that color when turned from it. The eye accustomed to the red of a woman's dress, unconsciously sees a greenish cast in the face that is naturally pale, and in the same way the pallor of a woman's face takes on a tint of red as the complement [Pg 92] or contrast of a green dress. As one's appetite for the thing that is sweet becomes exhausted by a superabundance of sweets, so the eye resting upon a mass of red in the dress of a woman fails to appreciate the red tint in the face, and the face thus juxtaposed becomes pallid. A red-faced woman often wears brighter red in dress, so that her face may appear less red. The blue dress gives yellow to the face; the yellow dress gives blue; these results are altered materially by the intervention of white between the face and the dress. White intensifies color. If there is a tinge of pink in the face white brings it out. If there is sallowness in the face white accentuates it. It is for this reason that many women wear

yellow instead of white at the neck, so that the yellow of the face becomes less conspicuous by contrast. (See ¶ 31.)

161. It is dangerous, however, in matters of dress to strictly apply this rule, because color has a temperamental influence apart from the purely visual. Some women are positively depressed by certain colors; such colors are to be avoided, no matter what the deductions of theory. (See ¶ 94.)

162. The black dress will make a woman look pale, for the reason that the black absorbs whatever color there may be in her face. A dark color has also absorbent characteristics. The lighter the color, the less absorbent. Hence light greens are preferable to bring out the color in the face than dark greens, assuming that we are to consider only this point, [Pg 93] which is all that is necessary to consider in house decoration. Therefore light greens as a background to theater boxes or as a wall background are always desirable.

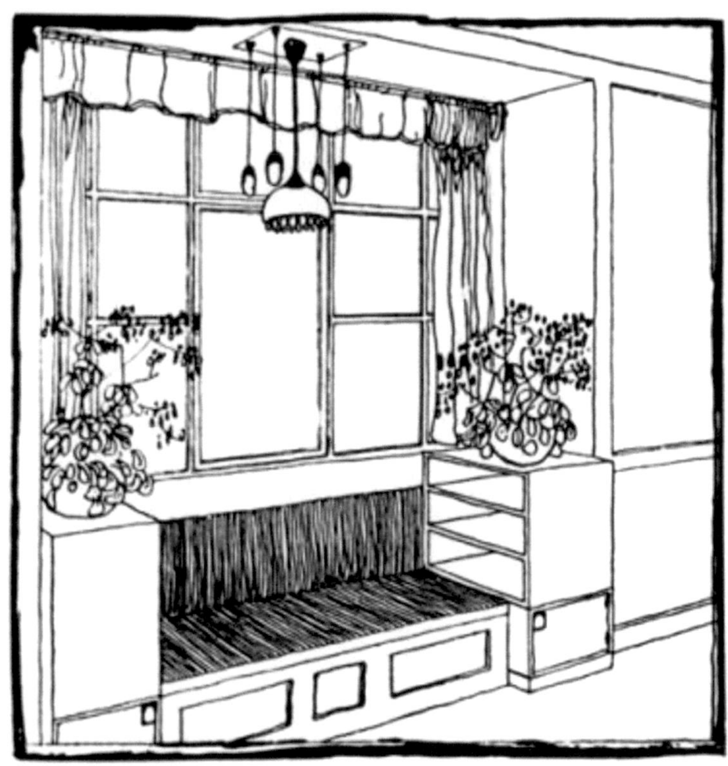

Lighting by wires. See ¶ 153.